Core Images
of the Self

Jean Dalby Clift

CORE IMAGES OF THE SELF

*A Symbolic Approach
to Healing and Wholeness*

CROSSROAD • NEW YORK

1992
The Crossroad Publishing Company
370 Lexington Avenue, New York, NY 10017

Printed in the United States of America

Library of Congress Cataloging-in-Publication Data

Clift, Jean Dalby.
    Core images of the self : a symbolic approach to healing and
wholeness / Jean Dalby Clift.
        p. cm.
    Includes bibliographical references and index.
    ISBN 0-8245-1218-9 (hard)
    1. Symbolism (Psychology)—Therapeutic use.   2. Imagery
(Psychology)—Therapeutic use.   3. Psychotherapy.   I. Title.
RC489..S93C5   1992
616.89'14—dc20   92–24560
                                                    CIP

To Wallace

Of all God's graces
this one high grace:
not to have had to live my life
without you.

Contents

Preface

My attempt in this book is to talk about symbols and their meanings in a way which will make that meaning more generally available. I am suggesting a process of exploring meaning, one that I hope will be adaptable to others regardless of whether they share my particular perspectives.

Everyone, of course, comes from a particular perspective, and we are happily past believing that our own views are universal. Mine is pastoral counseling, and this material was devised in my supervision groups and clinical work in pastoral counseling. Though I work primarily as a pastoral counselor and supervisor, I also act part of the time as a spiritual director, a teacher, and a parish priest. I myself remain in receipt of spiritual direction, as I have for a number of years. My own tradition is Christian, and my writing and work obviously have that basis, but I intend and hope that my own bias does not prevent its usefulness for others.

This material has been presented to three regional meetings of the American Association of Pastoral Counselors, to other groups of clinicians and spiritual directors, and a reflective form of the work has been the focus of retreats. I have also been able to try out these ideas on my family and friends, particularly my colleagues in the Denver Diplomate Training Group, to all of whom I acknowledge a warm debt of gratitude.

I have retained something of the informal style of oral presentations, frequently using language which is available to nonprofessionals. This runs the danger of lacking the precision of more technical language, but for me the gain is worth the loss, because I want to speak to two general types of audience. I hope core image work will prove helpful to my favorite character, the average intelligent person, and thus be of general usefulness. I have also written for clinicians and spiritual directors—people who work in the various helping professions to aid others.

Those interested primarily in the practical use of core images for their own inner work may wish to omit chapter 6, "Operational Theory" and chapter 7, "Diagnosis," both of which refer to somewhat more technical material. Chapter 9, containing more detailed case studies, is included mainly for people who learn by studying examples and might benefit from longer narratives.

Above all, I want to stress for all readers that core image work is a symbolic approach which can be used along with other ways of personal growth and healing. It is never intended to be exclusivist.

Lastly, I want to express public gratitude to the people who have graciously allowed me to share their core image material. Such a book as this could not, of course, exist without their generosity. They have been my teachers, and I have enjoyed the classes.

· PART I ·

Identifying Core Images

·1·

Symbols and Personality

Core images are the central symbols of our lives and of our personalities. We can probably never completely plumb their meaning for us, but we can learn to listen, especially to listen with "symbolic ears." If we can identify our core images, we will be in touch in a more conscious way with our central patterns. Any such increase in consciousness is helpful, of course, and core images are particularly so. They are clues to understanding and connecting with the events of our past, with our present thoughts, emotions, and behavior patterns, and even with the direction of our future. They put us in touch with ourselves at the deepest levels of personality and with the meaning of our lives, including our personal images of God.

The riddle of human personality is endlessly interesting, and the increase in the study of our own psychology is a dominant development of the twentieth century. Perhaps we have been forced to study ourselves primarily by the increasing technical power we can wield. As we see this power proliferate, we become painfully aware that we can destroy ourselves or not: the choice is up to human beings.

Why do we do the things we do? What makes us into the people we are? What can we do, if anything, to become different? Why are other people not like us? What makes us all tick? How will we use our power? How will those decisions be made? To explore how, it is crucial that we learn more about people, about our own psychology. What makes *us* "work"?

In the attempt to understand human personality, I suggest that we can learn far more about ourselves through the symbols of our lives than in any other way. We are symbolic creatures, and, in mysterious ways, our lives operate in symbolic patterns. Symbols are central to us as human beings.

We constantly encounter reality through symbols. Words themselves are symbols, of course, but even more, the only way we can comprehend ourselves and our lives is through symbols. Symbols are not simply an "extra" in life—something to reflect on if you have time for that sort of thing, like a hobby. They are in fact the way in which all of us function.

From the time my study of Jungian theory began in 1963 through all the various methods and techniques I have learned about since, I have increasingly come to the opinion that this symbolic approach to therapy and wellness is central and important. I first wrote about symbols in connection with work with dreams, and I still think that is important, but the more I worked, the more convinced I became that symbolic work was far broader than dream work, and—somehow—more *ordinary:* a common human experience which could be accessed for healing.

To access this symbolic work and its basic components in an ordinary way, I began to search for a descriptive phrase which would not annoy people the way that jargon does those unfamiliar with it, and yet which accurately expresses the meaning of the symbolic focus. The phrase I chose was "core images." I find repeatedly that people know when they hear it, at least in a general way, what I am talking about. It is a common-sense, ordinary phrase, easily available to the average intelligent person.

Symbolic understanding begins with the search for the core images in each person's life. The most important of them can last all our lives, continuing to unfold and reveal new levels of meaning to us, like threads that run all the way through a weaving. Others may be crucial to our lives for a while and then drop away, as if their purpose had now been served and they themselves incorporated into our inmost being.

We are probably all clusters of several such core images, and the description of them would be one way of understanding the total complexity that makes up any person. In fact, our very complexity can be understood symbolically by the way in which our core images are interwoven with one another. Whenever we find them, they are our carriers of meaning. They are the core components of spiritual growth and of the therapeutic task because they communicate our inner reality to us.

Novelists and playwrights have inherently known about core images. The core images of the characters' lives are what tie the novel or the play together. Composers of music know this, and the recurring musical themes are what tie a symphony together. They are also what say to the audience in the middle of an opera, "Oh, here comes that character again." This patterning in art, I would assert, is following life. Life is also like that, with its core images.

Core images will carry through in many phases of our lives. They are patterns of response and feeling, frequently very charged feelings. The emotions carry the value of the images for us, though in some instances the emotions have been so hidden in the unconscious that they are forgotten. These patterns of core images have the property of genuine symbols in that they can continue to teach and inform us, especially once we have consciously identified them.

Further, I think many contemporary theorists are really operating from symbolic modalities which are closely related to one another and thus can helpfully be understood under one umbrella. I myself am heavily indebted to Jungian theory, as will clearly appear. I think Jung probably taught us more about symbolic work than any other theorist, but I do not want to use analytical psychology in a limited, exclusive way. I am reaching for a way of pulling together whatever personality theories we have learned and of seeing them symbolically. I want to try to describe and define symbolic work in a more inclusive language and form.

We all need organizing structures in order to begin to understand ourselves and our lives. If an individual's core images are treated as an organizing structure, they will function more accurately to understand that individual's life than will some kind of synthetic organizing structure.

Even when we identify our core images, however, they are unclear, perhaps in part because of the charged quality of the emotion surrounding them. They present themselves in our lives, but where are they leading us? What do they teach us? This is not so clear and requires work and patience.

It is here that they call to mind the riddling oracles at Delphi in ancient Greece. In the eighth century B.C.E., the sanctuary of

Apollo in rural Greece rose to national prominence because so many state officials and private citizens came there seeking advice about what to do. The answers were given by a prophetess in a trance, thus making clear that what we would now call the unconscious realm was being accessed.

Many people have found it fascinating that the sanctuary of the god Apollo, the god of cool rational logic, should be the place where political and personal decisions came to depend on oracles from an altered state of consciousness. As the Hindus might say, I don't think that is an accident. I think some kind of balance was going on there which we might do well to pay attention to.

What brings these oracles to mind in connection with work with core images is their essentially ambiguous nature. The statements from the oracle could always be interpreted in more than one way. Cynics may say that this kept the oracle from ever being wrong, but I suggest that this ambiguity is precisely the point with core images.

The core images in our lives point us toward important patterns which are affecting us, but they do not tell us what to do about them. That is left to us. In that tension of possible choices lies the riddling mystery and sometimes an agonizing frustration as we try to discern which choice is good and creative, which choice is destructive. In that tension of choice is the possibility for change, even for transformation of some core images which have been perceived as quite negative into something positive for our lives. As the Ulanovs have put it, "The images that guide us are powerful. How we relate to them differentiates healing from harm."[1]

Such transformations are possible because the core images operate in the present, they reach back into our past, and, most crucially, they point toward our future. They point us toward the choices we face, toward our customary ways of dealing with life, toward the way we think about ourselves, and even toward new and creative possibilities.

Core images can be a helpful way of understanding ourselves and other people, for our own spiritual life and our relationships, even without specialized training. I also think that understanding core images can be useful for therapists and spiritual directors who work with other people. The examples of core images I will use are from various sources, including clinical practice, and I will also illustrate how to use them under the aegis of a clinical practice.

Defining Some Terms

I want to define some of the terms I use because, as T. S. Eliot has taught us, words slip and slide. We don't all use even common words to mean the same thing. Let me say first how I am using the word *symbol.* I use the word the way Jung does, I think, but Paul Tillich has the clearest method of expressing the meaning of a symbol, as he makes the important distinction between a symbol and a sign.[2] Tillich said signs point to something; they point to another reality. Symbols, like signs, also point to another reality, but in addition they *participate* in the reality to which they point. A symbol makes the other reality present. So a symbol has two aspects: a concrete aspect which is seen, and the other reality to which it points, which is unseen. As Christianity and most other religions assert in their beliefs, the unseen reality is far more significant and important than the seen reality.

We have seen a perfect example of symbol-sign acted out in the United States by the furor about burning the American flag. Now, if you burn the flag, you are, at one level, just burning a piece of cloth. If you were just burning a flag as a sign, then you would be burning a piece of cloth which points to something. It points out, for instance, that the building on which it hangs is a government building of the United States of America. If that is all the flag meant—pointing out, for example, where to find the post office—there would probably be no furor, and for that matter, there would probably be no burning.

But the flag is not just a sign; it is a symbol—both for the people who burn the flag and for the people who object to the burning. Both groups are using the flag to mean something much more than itself, more than the piece of cloth, more than the post office building; they are using the flag to point to the values for which it stands. Both sides care very much about what the country—and the flag—stand for. They are both using the flag, with great intensity, as the symbol for the country and its actions.

Yet only when a symbol is kept translucent does it function truly as a symbol. It might clarify this to point to another difference—that between an idol and an icon. Several world religions stress, coming out of the ten commandments, that worshipers are not to make idols and worship them. God is thus seen as beyond any possible physical representation, and seeing the physical representation *as* God is a violation of true relationship with God. On the other hand, an icon, particularly as the Orthodox Christian tradition uses it, is a way of seeing through some physical representation to the true God, so that an icon can lead one beyond itself to God. Symbols, truly seen, are like icons, not idols.

Now let me say what I mean by an *image*; here I use the word as literature defines it, with a slightly expanded use which I will mention later. In literature, especially in poetry, "image" has a specific meaning. An image in poetry is something concrete which communicates directly through the reader's senses. The concreteness is important because the image must carry directly from the writer to the reader in a manner which abstractions cannot do.

Concrete nouns make good images. If I say "rose," for example, or "tiger" or "Empire State Building," you see essentially the same sensory picture I do. Sensory details are not limited to the visual, but may also include other sense impressions—sometimes appealing to several senses at once. Because they also communicate clear sensory details, many action verbs are also good images—verbs such as "skipping" or "clapping."

Human communication operates most clearly at the level of images. Freud surmised that picture language precedes thinking in words, and it is this picture language which concrete images attempt to reproduce. Yet when an image is functioning symbolically, as it is in literature, it moves beyond its easily communicable, concrete reality to the symbolic use, to the other reality to which the symbol points, to what Tillich and Jung would emphasize: its participatory quality. We cannot speak about unseen, ultimate reality except by way of images—it is "as if . . ."; "it is like. . . ."

When this quality is accessed, then the symbol can talk of the unseen reality, the world of inner experiences, emotions, feelings, moods, and values. In each person's life, the concrete picture language of the images which appear are usually expanded into a story, a drama of inner meaning. These images both point to some personal pattern and continue to carry the life meaning forward, for good or ill. When these two qualities come together—the image patterns which appear in each life and the participatory significance of the image patterns—then I would say such images are central to our lives. They are *core images*.

Some Dangers to Avoid in Symbolic Work

In order to maintain a genuinely symbolic approach, there are some needed cautions—some "potholes" into which it is easy to fall on a symbolic journey. The materialistic side of us can easily take control in several ways.

The first pothole is thinking that if something is symbolic, then it is not real. Jung was very strong on this point. He said: never say, *"only* a symbol." Symbols are in fact, he argued, images of contents which transcend consciousness. He called the uniting quality of symbols their "transcendent function." These contents which the symbols carry are completely real; they are just unknown. In part this is because they always have two parts: the concrete image and the deeper meaning which the image holds and can make present to us.

Working with symbolic images comes more easily for some people than others, but symbolic language is probably our earliest human connection. In symbols the inner experiences, feelings, and thoughts are expressed *as if* they were experiences or events in the outer world. This is one reason artists and writers can communicate with others. They operate on the level of symbol, showing, as C. S. Lewis puts it, the "insides" on the outside. When our insides click with our outsides, we are shown something of ourselves, something we can resonate with. Those artists who capture the essence of the insides of a great many people speak to their own time, or perhaps to all time.

Another pothole—really, a chasm in the road—is concretizing the meaning of images. At its worst, this is the symbol book from the grocery store checkout line. A few years ago as a joke, my children stuffed my Christmas stocking with a little book called *A Dream Dictionary*, which tells you how to tell what the symbols in your dreams mean. This has such fascinating information as (in the "A" section) that if you dream of the ace of spades, you aren't being paid enough for your work and (in the "Z" section) that to dream that you take a child to the zoo predicts you will receive a lot of money. From A to Z that little book says dreams are about money, which I guess is how to appeal to the public today. This is a reifying of imagery, instead of staying with understanding the images as symbol.

The comparison which the symbol points to and participates in is never the same as the image; there is no absolute equation between image and meaning for everyone for all time. We cannot say that the meaning of a particular image *is* this-or-that, but we always need to say that it is *as if* this-or-that. The distinction is crucial.

It is very important not to reduce a symbol to some specified rational explanation. Reduction is the antithesis of what we must learn to do with symbols, which is let them continue to live and continue to inform us, communicate to us with power. We can never learn the meaning of symbols for our lives if we only reduce them to something else, or, as I suggested above, if we treat them as idols instead of icons. We can make associations and amplify the images, in fact get all the associations we can, but then we always know there is more.

My favorite image for this is the contemporary public relations release. When a printed release covers more than one page, at the bottom of each page, in capital letters, is the word MORE, to tell you to keep going. That is how it is with symbols. No matter how much meaning you have attached to a given image, you need always to see it with MORE in all caps at the end of the page.

What this shows us is that we are all more than cause and effect; the meaning of our life is captured in symbols, which always point toward "more." As one writer put it, "The metaphors and symbols at the core of our mini-narratives break open the horizon of their narratives to 'more,' and point to the dynamic character of experience, the condition of possibility that metaphors and symbols have meaning."[3] This "more" has to do with the richness of experience in the world, which always opens out and calls us on.

This aspect of the symbol—that it can never be completely grasped—Jung saw as the unconscious aspect. "As the mind explores the symbol," he said, "it is led to ideas that lie beyond the grasp of reason."[4]

Once we get accustomed to this idea, it should be familiar to religious folk, because our religious symbols also operate with many levels of meaning which carry us along to unknown depths of meaning the more we live with them. They, too, cannot be reduced to some specified rational explanation alone. They are living, and we need to let them live and continue to grow in our lives.

Another pothole is somewhat close to the danger of concretizing the image—the view that your images tell you what to do, or we might say, absolutizing the direction of the image. This pothole seems to arise particularly with reference to dreams. Once people begin to pay attention to dream imagery at all, they are likely to make an idol of the image, taking it to be the whole truth. Dreams give you information, and they *never* tell you what to do. The choice is always with you.

I arrive at the position that dreams never tell you what to do theologically, because I believe we are given freedom of choice, (not absolute, but nonetheless real) which freedom is central to our lives. That's the help the dreams are—to give us more information so we can make better choices. To reify the dream would be to say that one was doomed or destined to live one's life in a certain way, and that I do not believe.

As Shakespeare has one character in *King Lear* say, "When we are sick in fortune, we make guilty of our disasters the sun, the moon, and stars; as if we were villains on necessity, fools by heavenly compulsion . . . and all that we are evil in, by a divine thrusting on" (Edmund, act 1, scene 2).

Most of us are all too ready to turn over our decision-making to others and go helpless and be cared for. A wonderful contemporary image of this helplessness is portrayed on PBS in a series called "Mystery." They have different stories, sometimes Sherlock Holmes, sometimes Agatha Christie, sometimes Lord Peter Wimsey, or others.

The shows are always introduced by a set of cartoon scenes designed by Edward Gorey and Derek Lamb. Various mystery-related vignettes appear. In the first set, someone is shot and slides into a lake, a vulture cries and flaps away, detectives tiptoe after a wheelchair. On top of a wall, a woman lies on her back crying pitifully, "Ah, ah," drops a handkerchief on the head of some detectives stalking below the wall, and finally raises her hand to her head and sighs helplessly.

I had literally watched that show for months before I noticed that only her ankles are tied together. All she has to do is sit up, untie her ankles and get down from the wall. Or, if the knot is too hard for her, she's not gagged. She can lean over and call to the detectives, "Hey, guys, anybody got a pocket knife?" But instead she lies there, helplessly crying, "Ah, ah," and waiting to be rescued by someone else.

I use this on myself and the people I work with. Once, when my car died in cold weather and wouldn't restart, I got out on the street and was looking up and down—really probably for a knight on a white horse. When I caught myself, I said, "Ah, ah," put on my gloves and scarf, locked the car, and began hiking for someone to tow my car.

In the second set, which now introduces the series, the scenes have become even more chaotic. There is a driving rain storm and a large chunk falls off a wall. The woman is still on top of the wall, but the wall is much higher now, and parts of it are falling off. She still waves her arms and cries, "Ah, ah." She lets her scarf drop, but now the wind carries it away, and there is no one to hear her cry or find her scarf. Yet, still only her ankles are tied. Her situation is even more difficult, but she does have more choice than she knows.

This is an image of how we can move into a helpless victim role without recognizing that there are other options and that we can get out of it. When we are caught in something, it always seems as if we have no options, but there are always options. As Viktor Frankl has taught us, even in the death camps, there was still what he called "the last of the human freedoms," the ability "to choose one's attitude in any given set of circumstances, to choose one's own way."[5]

One woman told me after I had used this image in a weekend workshop that she went home and recorded this segment of the cartoon over and over about five times. Then, whenever she felt an attack of helplessness coming on, she played the video for herself.

The avoidance of such potholes as these needs to be the backdrop for all symbolic work.

Sources of Core Images

With these warnings in mind, we are ready to look for core images. They are found in many places, all connected with the "living human document" of the individual life. They are images and stories that linger in our minds. It is this lingering which points toward their significance for us. They can be images of beauty, like a rose window or a sunset or a particular mountain; they can be images of terror, or war, or accident, or death. They may be general images, but for us they become particular.

One major category of core images comes from memories from our life histories. Sometimes these images are the little stories or scenes which constitute our earliest memories. Sometimes they are traumatic; sometimes they are quite ordinary. Some Native American Indian cultures assigned people their true names, based on some significant event or image in their lives, as portrayed in the movie *Dances With Wolves*—in a way that is very similar to the way some core images come from our memories. For some people, such memories almost become their "true names."

Another fruitful source of core images is found in the family of origin: in family stories or in the family patterns which genograms reveal. We can find them in the "messages" our families gave us about life and in the roles we fulfilled in the family—usually only partly chosen by the child, mostly imposed by the needs of the family. The larger social dimension of our lives is also influential in giving us "messages" about ourselves which become dominant for us and which may be either helpful or destructive. Such images may be such a core part of our lives that they continue long after we have moved away from home or left the milieu that set them.

Interestingly, core images can frequently be found in stories—in stories we loved or hated as children. When we respond to such stories, they can become part of us, part of our personal mythology. This can include, if we were introduced to them, scripture stories or images that speak deeply to us, including our pictures of God. Poems, songs, or pictures which have remained in our minds despite their apparent triviality are sources for identifying core images. Several people from the "baby boomer" generation tell me firmly that their core images come from television—including the cartoons and even the advertising.

They can be discovered in dreams or other materials from the unconscious. Important dream images sometimes stay in our memory and consciousness long after waking, even sometimes for years. Such dream images are usually core components for us.

Psychosomatic medicine makes a connection between body and

psyche to show how closely integrated they are; this field generally suggests a causal connection between body and mind. It can be equally (or even more) helpful to view symptom as symbol. Pioneering work in this field came when Aarne Siirala taught us to give illness a voice and listen to its meaning.[6] Not only physical symptoms, but those in addiction may contain such otherwise voiceless core images. Many observers study the form of addiction in its specificity to see the essentially symbolic nature or meaning in the addiction.

A powerful source of core images is sexual fantasy. Sexuality is such a powerful force in our lives that no one is without sexual fantasies, even if not caught in the sexual obsessions so prevalent in our time. The specific nature of a particular sexual fantasy can be studied for clues to core images. Where, for example, does the fantasy occur—in prison, in church, in a foreign country? Take this and other specific details to examine the symbolic world of longing or fear.

In fact, any experience of the unconscious impinging on consciousness can be a clue to a core image. So-called Freudian slips can be examined as to their subject matter or nature to discover something of which we are not consciously aware, and this subject matter may well contain a core image. Even the spontaneous images of our fantasies can contain core images, whether they are visions, hallucinations, or apparently idle fancies.

Once we enter into a process of self-reflection, either alone or with someone to help us, we find many sources. We can find them in body language, in distortions of how we define certain words such as "love" and "marriage," in synchronicities and intuitions of meaning, even in the irrational dissonances in our lives—in any of the material that goes to make each of us who we are. In spiritual direction or therapy, they can be found in complexes, in free associations, in the dynamics of interpersonal responses, in transference and countertransference, or in parallel processes between client and therapist.

Wherever they are found, they are the basic symbols of our lives, and as such they have much to teach us.

The next chapters will give examples of some case histories of some of the main ways we can identify our core images, some of the more common places where we encounter them, and how they can be understood to speak to us of our past, present, and future.

·2·

Memories

A pioneer pastoral counselor once told me that in her training the one thing her teachers would never let her forget to ask was, What is your earliest memory? Depth psychology has always considered one's earliest memory as having special importance for our lives.

It is easy to justify this emphasis. If the event doesn't have some continuing significance for us, why do we remember this particular memory? Sometimes the answer is clear, because the memory is so traumatic. Other times the memories seem casual, almost accidental, but they are always symbolically important. They may even be parts of our family history that we are not quite sure we remember. Maybe we have only heard about them, but because we were told so much about them, they have somehow become part of us as well.

Memories are strange and wonderful and terrible. They are one of the most powerful sources of tracing our core images. In core image work, we work with our memories not just to belabor them, but to begin to see the ways in which our lives are stories, with patterns and themes and "signals."

Contemporary author Frederick Buechner, in writing his own autobiographical works, encourages all of us to listen back over our lives, pointing out, "memory is more than a looking back to a time that is no longer; it is a looking out into another kind of time altogether where everything that ever was continues not just to be, but to grow and change with the life that is in it still."[1]

This listening and looking back is itself a religious task when it genuinely engages to be as truthful as it can be. If not, it is a frivolous plaything or an exercise in deception. As we look at our memories as truly as we can, we are looking at what one writer has called "an intriguing tension between the moral demands for consistency and stability and integrity of character, and the constant awareness of psychological complexity and ambiguity in self-knowledge."[2] In other words, the writing of a continuing autobiography can be a way of clarifying for ourselves "everything that ever was" in our own lives.

It is in that sense of memory that I want to speak about core images that come to us from our memories, using some examples I have been given permission to use. Such memories and family tales are wonderful clues to the patterns that mold us and influence our behavior and attitudes and how we think about ourselves. They can be significant far beyond their apparent importance at the time. The first example I use is one which seemed quite small, but which returned to memory—almost casually—in therapy.

A Child's Taped Mouth

A woman, whom I will call Laura, has given me this story and its aftermath to use. She was in her fifties when she entered therapy, but her primary core image comes from an early life experience when she was a toddler. Her mother evidently had a friend over for tea one day, and the little girl was bothering the women as they tried to talk. In exasperation, the mother turned to Laura and said something like, "If you don't hush and stop chattering, I'm going to tape up your mouth."

Laura left the room for a few minutes and when she returned, she had found the tape and taped her own mouth closed. She showed it to her mother—trying to please her, I am sure. It's not particularly traumatic; it's just a funny childhood incident, one which got repeated because it was so precocious. However, in adulthood, in therapy, Laura came to see that it can be understood as a core image of how she has lived her life. This is *not* to say that the incident necessarily *caused* Laura to develop as she has, but simply to say that the incident points to her way of being. I am far less interested in cause than in the effect of this patterned way of being on her life. When you're in your fifties, taping up your mouth is not so cute anymore. It can distort your whole life.

When Laura entered therapy, she listed three goals that she had for her therapy. As I tell them, think of each one against the background image of her taping up her mouth. Her first goal was to release her creativity, which she felt she couldn't get a handle on; she felt strained whenever she tried to let her creativity out and feared that this just meant she was not capable of any kind of creativity.

The second goal was to get rid of her fear, which she lived with all the time. She said she had so much anxiety that it was like a constant cloud over her. You may remember a cartoon character named Joe Bftsplk, the man in *Li'l Abner* who walked around under a continual rain cloud. She felt like that.

The third concern was also one of fear: she was so afraid of others' anger that she continually manipulated herself into trying to avoid making anyone angry. In fact, she came to see that she was so afraid that she tried to maintain iron control over every life situation in order to avoid any of the things she was afraid of.

Do you hear the resonance with that core image? You could express each one of her goals as if from the toddler with tape still on her mouth—only now writ large and become a way of life for the grown woman, blocking her from her life and creativity.

Incidentally, one thing which pushed her into continuing therapy was a couple of requests she had received to serve as the spiritual director for others. She felt she was being called into the work, and she had been trained for it, but—to express her problem in terms of the image—how can you be a spiritual director with tape on your mouth from trying to please others?

Just after she decided to enter therapy, she had a dream, which also points her toward the work she needs to do:

> There was a fire—it approached from a short distance away from another house or other houses—there was a reddish vapor that ignited—tall trees—they would glow, but not necessarily burn. It seems like I had a concern about it, but not undue fear—and it was finally like I needed to decide what needed to be saved— going through things was going on while the house was burning.

This fire which burns but does not consume had a religious association for her. She connected it with a biblical passage in Isaiah about passing through the flame, but not being burned. She saw it as a direction to decide what was important for her, to do some sorting out, and in the dream she seems able to do that quite calmly without the fear with which she usually approached life.

Another biblical image which comes to mind, of course, is the bush which burned but was not consumed which caused Moses to turn aside and receive his call from God. In Laura's case, the fire is getting near her, so it is time to begin her sorting.

Various related themes appeared early in her therapy work as she began to sort through her "house." She described a continual horrible sense of inadequacy. She had always felt that she wasn't smart and was shocked when she was closing up her mother's house to find her old report cards and see that she had, literally, made all As and Bs through school, a fact she had totally forgotten. Her sense of her own intelligence and ability was not in accordance with objective reality.

She wanted to do some scripture teaching in her church community, but felt she dared not do so, because she wasn't capable. She said when she tried to speak up, especially if she wanted to disagree with someone, her heart would pound, sometimes so hard that she would blank out and forget what she had to say. Then she again felt as dumb as her memory told her she was. The tape was on her mouth; she needed to please.

Yet when she didn't speak up, she became depressed and felt helpless, as if life could never really be alive and vital. Once when she was in an argument with her husband, she realized she was mad because she felt she was "not being heard." She said the feeling was so strong that she felt nonexistent, as if she were being annihilated.

And she was! And she was participating in doing it—still carrying out her funny little attempt to please her mother and get approval. By living with this pattern of hers and building up the protection all through the years, she had managed to close down her life, but life will not stand for it. It demands to be let out in some way. Her ways of letting it out were to try to hold it in until it burst out in some uncontrollable anger or squirmed out in sneaky manipulation and innuendo. We will not stand for our own annihilation.

Another way of identifying what I am talking about, of course, is to say she has identified one of her complexes. The advantage of thinking in such a term as "core image" is that it stresses the individual nature of the complex. You could say this was a mother complex or even an authority complex or an inferiority complex, and all of these would be true. But I find it helpful to think in the specific terms of identifying core images which arise out of each life situation, precisely because they are so specific to the person.

Several clues indicate that this is a core image for Laura. The first is her continuing memory of the incident, though it is apparently so trivial. Usually, intensity of feeling is a clue, but here there is no direct connection between Laura's feelings and the image. She had managed effectively to stuff her feelings about this incident and its aftermath. The intensity of feeling came back to her only as she tried to take the tape off—in the dry-mouthed terror she felt at speaking up.

In Laura's case, identifying the core image came, first, with the fact that she remembered and repeated it, and second, in the explanatory or interpretive role which the core image carried. It had not come out as a part of her original history at the beginning of therapy, but only a little later as she spoke of having always known that her brother was her mother's favorite child, so that she was always trying to please her mother. So the family dynamics about which Laura felt great sadness and some hidden anger called attention to this vignette as a snapshot of how Laura fit into the world of her family of origin. This memory image summed it up.

As she worked with it, her feelings could all be interpreted, as we have seen, as aspects of a toddler with tape on her mouth. The more she worked with these connections, the more meanings she saw in it. So the utility of the image in understanding her own behaviors is a confirmation of its core significance for her.

It even pointed her toward her own desire to try to control life. When we first hear Laura's image, it seems pitiful, and it is; but it is also, on the other side, a toddler's grab for power. She will keep control as best she can, even if a part of the way she keeps control is by controlling her own behavior in order to please her mother. This problem was exacerbated in her life by her mother's chronic illness—all of which went together to make Laura overresponsible and afraid of conflict for fear of rejection.

In the adult, this pattern was still present, probably even

stronger. As an adult Laura was able to name in herself an even more tainted grab for power—manipulation, innuendo, and when it breaks out, a witchlike, ineffectual wrath. It looks like Laura is being agreeable; below that it looks like she is keeping control. In the grown woman, as Laura came to see, it is really neither. It serves to chip away at the possibility of creativity in her own life.

She saw that she had what she called a "deep and deadly habit of response" to life of trying to control it. Yet when she tried to control, she set herself up to be disappointed. Her own self-rejection, her own taping of her mouth, invited rejection, and she was stuck in a limited space. For her, a "larger" place, one with room to grow and live joyfully, came when she could take risks and be vulnerable despite her fears.

Using this core image, slowly, painfully, Laura began to risk speaking up about what she thinks, feels, believes. When she first began, she said her mouth felt dry after every time; but the need to articulate herself instead of letting it build up in rage was strong in her. She even began to realize that *not* speaking up clearly is part of what got her into traps with others. She was getting the tape off her mouth. By grace she could choose not to stay closed in and closed down and taped up.

Toward the end of our work, she delighted me by bringing in a snapshot of herself, which she insisted no one else was to see "because it looked so silly." It was taken at a conference where she had a leadership position. She knew I would love it because the photographer had caught her laughing at something, and her mouth was as wide open as a mouth could be. The core image was portrayed in a kind of healing.

As an outward symbol of this, she bought herself a little storyteller doll. These are dolls made by a southwest tribe of Native American Indians. They are shown with their mouths wide open and usually with a number of children gathered around listening to the storyteller passing on the history of the tribe. Laura's storyteller had become the symbol of the redemption of her taped mouth.

The core image is also frequently parallel to the client's picture of God. In Laura's case, a breakthrough of insight came when she saw that she behaved as if God were punitive, a view she consciously rejected. When the taped-mouth image grabbed her, she said, "then God is like Mother, who will punish me if I do anything wrong." Her fear of retribution if she took the tape off was like her fear of a retributional God. Her God of the core image was a God of fear, not a God she felt one could have faith *in*.

The two then went hand in hand: her work with trying to learn to speak up before the backlog of repressed energy made her explode and her ability to trust in a God who was not waiting around to punish her. She could then, tentatively at first, but with increasing strength, speak up with genuine peace.

Her core image work brought up part of her past to explain her present behavior, and it also pointed the way to its own healing and transformation. The healing pattern was inherent in the patterning of the wounding.

The Gift That Burns

Important core images are sometimes based on early traumas which affect the way life is viewed ever afterwards. A woman I will call Sarah came up to speak with me after I gave a talk on core images and told me that her core image was from her first memory. On her first birthday, she reached out to touch the one candle on her little cake and burned the index finger on her right hand. As she put it, "I was betrayed by my own birthday cake—something that was intended for my pleasure and celebration."

This pattern continued, in a far more serious vein, when, around the age of two, she was "burned" by her own father. She said that he was someone who was intended to be a celebration and place of safety for her, but he began to abuse her sexually. This sexual abuse and victimization continued, as she was burned by her own family. Oddly, she even remembers that she set a fire in the church nursery at around age seven.

Sarah described how this pattern continued through life and how it began to turn around:

> This theme carries on as I chose to marry a man—a Pastor—
> who then is sexually, physically, and emotionally abusive to
> me—betrayal by my own husband, who is supposed to bring
> celebration to marriage and be safe at home. Other men followed

after my marriage who also abused my trust—a seminary profes-
sor, for instance, who was supposed to be safe—betrayal again.
    I learned also to betray myself by setting up and sabotaging
myself to fail and "burn myself"—
    The transformation into the creative opposite occurs now as
I reclaim the sacredness of the flame while in meditation and
prayer times I use candles as therapeutic light. I imagine light
flowing through my body in healing of the dark corners. I find
a flame of light fascinating as it burns, consuming the wick.
    The core image of a single birthday candle has now provided
healing. I have candles throughout my house to warm my space,
to make my home. The core image is also the source of my
recovery as I have befriended it.

She added that now whenever she burns her finger, she wonders
what she needs to learn or pay attention to. She even remembered
to send me this story, as she had offered to do several months
before, when she burned that same index finger on a microwave
dish. She wrote, "I was rushing and in my haste I did not take care
of myself properly. I think I'm being called to slow down."
    Sarah's story illustrates well the way in which the core image
carries through in small things and large, and, of course, through
destructive experiences to recovery.

The Lost Refugee Child

A powerful core image from another early trauma was given me
to share by a recently ordained Methodist seminary student in an
intensive journal course. She said that as soon as she heard the
phrase "core image," she was back in her imagination to a trauma
she had at age three. The student, whom I will call Hedda, was
born in Poland, the German granddaughter of a Baptist minister,
in one of those areas of Europe that has changed national hands so
much that, she said, though she, her sister three years older, and
her mother were all born in the same town, her mother's birth
certificate is in Russian, her sister's in Polish, and hers in German,
with a swastika on it, for she was born during the Nazi regime.
    When she was three, her family began trying to escape, with
hundreds of other displaced persons—to escape, as she put it, from
the Russians, Poles, war, hunger, and fear. She called it "fleeing

their Egypt." The only vehicle they had was a covered wagon pulled by oxen. One day in Czechoslovakia, in subzero weather, her parents left Hedda and her sister with their grandmother while they went to look for food. Her grandmother fell asleep, and the two little girls slipped away. Hedda became fascinated with a German shepherd dog, chained and barking, so that when her sister said, "We'd better get back," she turned too late—in time to see her sister disappearing from sight between two wagons.

She was lost for what she called "an eternal half day." When people tried to help her and asked for her name, she wouldn't give it. Had she perhaps been warned not to talk to strangers? She said experiencing that hell of loss and separation is her earliest memory. She was finally found in the mass of fleeing refugees, and her father led them to East Germany, and just before the fall of the iron curtain, to West Germany, and then finally to the "land flowing with milk and honey," as she called it, the United States.

She saw this experience of being lost as the core image she had lived with all her life, and it took on religious overtones for her. She remembered wanting to be a minister growing up, though she mentioned it little, since "girls did not become ministers." She yearned for a sign, wanting, as she wrote: "a Saul/Paul sign; struck by light, slain by Spirit sign; God wants YOU to do THIS sign; unmistakable, hand of, voice of God sign; miraculous, awesome, only-God-could-do-this sign. I never got it."

She married, had a son, held positions of authority in government, worked for equal rights for women, divorced, and burned out. During all this, she struggled with a sense of being lost from God. Her personal picture of God was painted with the personal experience which most affected her.

You will have probably perceived that she has poetic ability, and she became a poet, as well as a minister. The first poem she ever wrote, seven years before the journal class, was a way of working through the connections with her core image of being lost. The first stanza of the poem is from the three-year-old point of view. The words are all one syllable, and the view is from the height of a three year old.

> Lost
> I was three
> and I was

lost
Big dog
on chain
in front of me
Ice, sun,
ox carts
on all sides
In my soul
fear
Boots, pants
skirts, muffs,
shawls and scarfs
Red ears
crisp breath
Blue eyes
brown eyes
eyes that probe
that pity
that fear
No Helga
No Mammi,
Pappi
Just bark
Bark bark
My name?
I won't tell you
I'll tell Pappi
my name,
not you
And then
the tears

[then the second stanza, the adult reflecting on the sense of still being lost]

Lost
I get lost
still
How do
I get to

Ash Street?
What shall
I be when
I grow up?
How do
I find You,
God?

Even without knowing more about Hedda's journey to find herself and God, we know that the journey led her to seminary and
to ordination, as if she "once was lost, but now is found."

Free to Supervise

The memories which continue to affect us do not always come
from childhood memories. An experienced counselor in a supervision group was something of a puzzle to the rest of the group
because she kept describing herself as a poor supervisor. In the
group the various members took turns bringing material from their
supervisory work, including audiotapes of sessions where they had
supervised other counselors. Such supervision is a means of continuing professional accountability. Other professionals have a
chance to raise questions, make suggestions, and generally both
criticize and commend one another.

Anyone who is chosen to supervise other counselors has already
achieved a high level of skill in counseling to the point where they
are ready to help others develop their own skills. Such was the case
with this experienced counselor, whom I will call Constance. The
other members of the group had heard several accounts of supervisory sessions and even tapes of those sessions where Constance was
supervising. They could hear the high level of her competence, yet
she herself, though usually a clear-sighted person, continued to
maintain that she was not a good supervisor.

When there is such a discrepancy between objective assessment
and subjective, personal assessment, there is usually something unconscious distorting the personal assessment. Many times with
women, one finds the cultural devaluing of women to be such a
factor; many women have internalized the centuries of thinking

women to be less than capable and so they judge themselves incapable. This did not seem to be the case with Constance, who was a mature, competent counselor and knew it. The discrepancy in her self-perception seemed to be limited to supervision.

Finally one day, in a breakthrough as the group puzzled over the issue, Constance "remembered" her first supervision experience. It was not really that she had forgotten the experience, but she had never identified its significance for her.

When Constance was in graduate school years before in another state, she was assigned a younger student to supervise as part of her training. This student became secretly angry at Constance because she wanted more time and attention than Constance gave her. She broke into Constance's office and completely trashed it, even stealing some of her files and generally wreaking havoc everywhere.

Anyone who has been robbed or had his or her space so invaded and wrecked knows the traumatic effect of it, and Constance realized that her resistance to supervising began right then. It is as if something in her closed down and just said, "I don't need this, but you can't always see it coming—so I'll just stay safe. I'll decide unconsciously not to supervise."

Constance, despite her level of professional experience, was operating out of a suppressed memory which tried to steer her out of danger by avoiding supervision. Once she realized where her negative assessment of herself was really coming from, the way was pointed beyond it. She beamed with pleasure at her new freedom to supervise and to perceive herself truly as doing it well.

The Concentration Camp

A colleague of mine in the American Association of Pastoral Counselors (AAPC), Han van den Blink, has developed some interesting and helpful theories about psychosystems, and he has spoken about his theories and the way in which his early life story contributed to the development of his theory. I trust his material will soon be published so as to be more widely available.

Han and I have had some interesting exchanges around the material each of us is working on. When I presented my material on core images in 1990 at AAPC's eastern regional meeting, I had not heard Han's material. It is copyrighted by Han, but he has given me permission to share both part of his material and the aftermath of his hearing me talk about core images.

Han's presentation of his psychosystems theory begins with a personal experience, which I quote in part:

> One morning last summer I went downstairs to get the mail. I made myself a cup of coffee and sat at the kitchen table to sort through the letters and magazines that had come in. My eye fell on a familiar manilla envelope, mailed from the Netherlands and addressed to me in my father's handwriting. He regularly sent me clippings or articles that he thought I might be interested in.
>
> One of the items in the manilla envelope was a recent copy of *Moesson* (Monsoon), a magazine for people like my parents who had lived and worked in Indonesia when it was still a Dutch colony, or for people who had been born there, and had been forced to leave in the late forties and early fifties after the Indonesians defeated the Dutch and achieved their independence.
>
> *Moesson* is full of nostalgic reminiscences and photographs of *tempo doeloe* ("the old days"), the fondly remembered past before the Second World War, when life was good for the Dutch and Eurasians who lived in that beautiful part of the world. In the last years, however, more and more articles have begun to appear with descriptions of personal, often harrowing, experiences during the War and its aftermath. There is widespread revival of interest in the Second World War, and after many years of silence, survivors are beginning to share what they have gone through.
>
> I was born in Java, one of the main islands of Indonesia, during the waning days of the Dutch colonial empire. As newlyweds my parents had left their native Holland for the Netherlands East Indies, as Indonesia was then called. There my father launched a successful career in education. When he later felt called to the ministry, our family left Indonesia for the United States where father got his thelogical credentials. We returned as soon as he got his degree. The outbreak of the hostilities with Japan in December, 1941 found us in Singapore where my father had become the minister of the Dutch speaking congregation.
>
> Few people at that time expected the war to last long, but the rapid deterioration of the situation in Singapore forced us to flee to what we hoped would be the safe haven of Java. It was not. The superior Japanese forces soon swept over the whole Indonesian archipelago and reached the very threshold of Australia.

Not long thereafter the internment of all Dutch civilians and others who were considered enemy aliens began, and we were put in a succession of worsening concentration camps.

In 1945, after my eleventh birthday, I was transferred like all other boys who had reached that age, to a separate encampment for men. That was the worst place of all, a hell hole that I despaired getting out of alive. I was there when the atomic bombs on Hiroshima and Nagasaki brought the war with Japan to an abrupt halt.

Leafing through *Moesson* I did not right away see the section my father had marked for me to read. When I did, I recognized the name of that last concentration camp I had been in, a name that had not often been in my conscious mind. The headline over the brief article read "Monument Boys Concentration Camps Bangkong-Gedunjati 1944–45" and next to it was a photograph of a statue of a young emaciated boy, about twelve years old, clad only in a loincloth, and carrying a hoe and pickaxe. This small stark life-sized sculpture was going to be placed in Kaliabanteng, the cemetary where those who had died in that camp were buried.

My reaction was immediate and extraordinary. I felt as if I had been physically hit. It was as if the scab of some deeply hidden wound had been ripped off. I burst into tears and wept and wept as I kept looking at that picture and at that article. I could not stop crying. I was vaguely aware that my eyes widened, as in fright, and that the sound I was making was not that of a grown man crying but that of a much younger person, a boy.

I sat at the kitchen table for a very long time, weeping and sobbing and staring at that well-known and awful name, and at that poor boy who stood for me and for so many others whom I had known. I was flooded with feelings and images of that dreaded camp, of the suffering and despair, of the starvation, of the abuse, and of the feelings of helplessness. It amazed me how sharp and immediate these feelings were, as fresh as if they had happened yesterday, even though the events that occasioned them occurred more than forty years ago.

I became aware of another sensation. At first it was difficult to put a name to it. I can only describe it as a sense of vindication. *Finally* it was being admitted, publicly, how awful that experience had been, how much suffering had taken place, and how many young lives had been wasted or permanently scarred.

That bronze statue, with the inscription "Zij Waren Nog Zo Jong" (They Were Still So Young), acknowledged that what my fellows and I had gone through had really happened. That modest sculpture recognized that our suffering too was real. It was as if some burden was lifted, one that I was not even aware of having carried all these years. I felt strangely lighter.

Han goes on in his excellent paper to present a psychosystems perspective for pastoral counseling, but I have represented this much of his story in order to tell you what happened to Han later, when I spoke on core images at that eastern regional meeting.

Han came up to me after my first talk on Friday evening and shared what he had experienced as I described core images. He said he was instantly and intensely aware of an experience he had as the war ended. He said part of the memory might be faulty, but his image of himself was that he woke one morning and everyone was gone from the camp, and he was alone.

He said he had always had a good sense of direction, and he set out to find the women's camp and his mother. He walked several miles through the town to the other side and people would avoid him, dirty, emaciated, in rags, as he walked. He remembers arriving at the gate of the women's prison and hearing someone call his mother's name excitedly, saying, "Han is here. Han is here." Then he collapsed and remembers no more.

He told me that night that he was sure in his being that this scene somehow was his core image and promised to send me his paper, which he later did. As I read it, moved by the suffering and tragedy of so many who were "still so young" and by Han's core image from the end of the war, I began to reflect on what the core image could be saying about Han and his life.

At the time I first heard his story, I knew very little of Han except my experience of him, which was as a robust, vibrant man, but one with a kind of inner stillness or peace about him, which is appealing and comforting to be around. As I speculated about the meaning this core image of his pointed to, it seemed to me that this moment—the moment when he heard his mother's name called—after the horror his young life had been through must have spoken to him as if to say: "Help is here now. Redemption is possible." Or, in the gospel language, you are saved. The voice calling out his mother's name and his enabled him to relax his incredible effort, resting, if you will, in saving arms.

It seemed to me that this virtue of hope then became a core reality for him, and it made sense that he could afterward carry out a ministry in pastoral counseling, holding out that hope to others. He is a wounded healer who knows we can escape from the prisons of our lives into safety. So the choices Han had made with his life by becoming a pastor, a pastoral counselor, and a teacher of other pastoral counselors demonstrate the core significance of this formative life experience.

He was also thus singularly situated to understand that not all psychotherapy can be based on the internal workings of an individual, and thus to see systems theory as a helpful, even necessary, adjunct to working with problems, which never arise in isolation. Because he was a child without power, subjected to a tortured young life by forces far outside himself, he sees the individual relationally—both as to the cause of trauma and also, because of his saving experience at the end of the war, as to the solutions. By listening to his core image account, I was able to speculate about the theological underpinning of his life. When I checked this out with him, he strongly affirmed my theological reflection about the meaning of his core image in his life.

So a reflection about the meaning and course of our lives can begin with core memories—whether they are seemingly trivial ones like Laura's or traumatic ones like Hedda's or Han's, whether early memories like Sarah's or late ones like Constance's—whatever comes to mind. It is usually helpful to write down the memory with all the details you can recall, especially the emotional ones, because those are important clues for the meaning and significance of the images for you.

Then the unfolding of the image as it lives on in our awareness can remain a source of consciousness and growth, particularly in the way the image can point toward our particular freedom from the past and toward our healing and wholeness.

·3·

Community and Family

*A*nother excellent source of core images is a study of the patterns in the family, especially in the family genogram. It really is true that the sins of the parents are visited upon the children for generations, especially the most sensitive of the children.

Beyond the family, we are all, of course, influenced by the other people with whom our lives are linked; and beyond individuals we know, we are all affected by the various elements of the contexts in which we live, the community, government, social patterns, religious institutions, and all the myriad social systems of our lives.

Systems theorists and social psychologists have given us helpful maps of this territory, and I suggest that symbolic work with core images ties in well with them. They are sources of identifying core images and can help us see ways to work with our particular image patterns, even very old ones. Jung once commented in a letter, "Our life is not made entirely by ourselves. The main bulk of it is brought into existence out of sources that are hidden to us. Even complexes can start a century or more before a man is born."[1]

Fire and Creativity

The current work with addictive and dysfunctional families is an exciting addition to any therapist's theoretical repertoire. Linda Leonard, a Jungian analyst in San Francisco, has worked on the archetypal patterns underlying addiction, illustrating the essential symbolic patterns in addictive families. Her recent book on creativity and addiction begins with her own experience in an alcoholic family, the history of which, she says, "was shrouded in the dark romance of alcohol."[2] As a child, she experienced all the "shame and horrors of addiction," but at the same time felt in her family history the "overwhelming figure of the Romantic in addiction."

Both her grandfathers and her father were alcoholics, and she says that in her whole family almost all the men are alcoholics and all the women but two married alcoholics. Of those two exceptions, one married a gambler and the other became a nun. She has worked with the romance of the image of the "happy drunk" side (of the family) in her mother's family to identify the way in which the codependence of these women functions.

Even more startlingly, on her father's side of the family, which she calls the "mean drunk" side, the image of fire was at the core of the family history. Her father's father "died by fire during a drunken debauch when the stove in his room overturned. Repeating death by fire, [her] father accidentally burned down the house when a cigarette fell from his hand while he was drunk, and [her] grandmother was killed."

She describes addiction in its archetypal aspects as a confusing process "in which the sufferer ceases to think clearly and to feel the genuine impulses of the heart." By working with the images of romance and fire, Leonard has used her own family's intergenerational core images to understand her own creativity. Because the addictive patterns are so prevalent in today's culture, her core images have a universalizing helpfulness.

Leonard had to face all this family material when she repeated it. Waking up in a detox ward, facing death, she reached her own abyss. She said all her fears and terrors were "rekindled, my past securities devoured in the blazing fire," but she also heard "the call to life." It was then she felt drawn into writing a new book, one about the very addiction which had almost killed her. She reports the dream that led to the book:

> I dreamt of an arsonist, an angry red-haired rebellious man, who threatened to burn down my retreat, a log cabin nestled in the dark quiet of the woods. I was angry too. I reacted by resentfully telling this man to "burn the house down." Flippantly he tossed a match into the house, setting the place ablaze. I realized that

I would be held responsible for the fire, for I held in my hands an implicating book. Then out of the house came a kindly man, who showed me a book cover—with the word *Witness* printed boldly on it. It was he who saved the house from burning down. From this dream came the title of this book.[3]

"Witness" for her referred to survivors, and she argues that the constructive fire within is the archetype of creativity. When her own inner fire wanted to be expressed, it came out in writing, but when she wrote her first book she says she was still caught in the family pattern of alcohol. It seems almost unbelievable to me, but she wrote it in a wine bar, writing some every night while she drank. It took her seven years. She thinks addicts can flee from the hellfire of addiction into the fire of the creative process, including the "purging fire of spiritual recovery" and the work to recreate themselves anew.

As she herself got free of the family pattern, her writing has also been freed into a purer creative fire. She has now written a striking book comparing the process of creativity to twelve-step programs, as part of her own process of creativity. The overcoming of addictions is like the process of creating the new art work of the recovering addict herself. As she uses her fire to create—books and herself—she sees that the core image of the fire in her family has pointed the way to the recovery. The core image has the possibility every day to lead to creativity or destruction, and this knowledge, together with the higher power acknowledged in the twelve-step programs enables her to choose the serenity—and fire—of recovery.

Again, the core images themselves—romance and fire—have pointed the way to her healing and recovery, and the family patterning showed this to her.

Sacrifice and Grounding

As Linda Leonard's core image came more and more clear to her from her family history, reflection on the dysfunctional aspects, and her own striking dream, Ken's came to him from a life crisis which led him into therapy and the subsequent insight he gained from looking at his family history.

Ken came into counseling at age fifty-two following a physical and emotional crisis in his life. A priest, he broke down at the altar in the midst of a service with crying he could not control. The matters that he related during his first counseling session were major clues to his core image patterns.

This crying episode followed shortly after a series of physical problems: pneumonia for five months, severe back trouble diagnosed as connected with overwork and requiring travel in a wheelchair, and spasms culminating in an episode with chest pains which ended with him in the emergency ward.

After these various physical ailments followed one another in such rapid succession and after his crying so hard during the service, his bishop recommended that he seek counseling, describing him as a "great absorber." Ken himself in his first counseling session described feeling as if the ground of his being was washing away.

He said he knew something was stored up in him—"I don't think I'm crazy," he said, but he knew he was not as together as he needed to be. He had experienced depression and heaviness, like a "dead weight," particularly the day before the Sunday episode.

He saw at once that he was worn out because he tried to be the in-between, the savior for people. "I really want people to all be OK," he said. After some conversation about the boundaries which he exceeded and how Ken achieved his self-esteem, it was suggested to him that he was talking about a pattern which was long established in his way of meeting the world.

Ken then immediately began to reminisce about his family of origin. He was the youngest of five children in a devout Roman Catholic family. When he was a year old, one of his next oldest sisters, a twin, died at four years old. Ken said, "My Mother cried for years for that loss." At six—"or probably earlier"—Ken began shielding his mother, as he put it, "deeply." In the eighth grade he remembered thinking: "How can I help my Mother through the change of life?"

Ken then casually remarked that he had almost died at birth. He had repeatedly been told that his father was asked by the doctor whether to save his wife or the baby, to which he replied, "By all means—my wife!" He said he honestly didn't feel any emotion about that.

When the therapist said that just wasn't possible, he reported that he did feel hurt by the surviving twin sister, who always picked on him. He said it had always *hurt* him when she hurt people with her quick tongue. Ken had stammered as a child and young man. A psychiatrist investigating his stammer in his early twenties asked him, "Is there anything that really bothers you?" He burst into tears and spoke of his sister's quick tongue.

He also remembered parenting his parents, especially when they would argue, and he would try to make peace between them. He had followed this pattern throughout his ministry. He said when someone would say something hurtful to someone else, he would experience his worst pain. He remembered, for example, being on a holiday on the beach of the river in Memphis when a posse went by with guns. One of the posse said, "We're going to get that nigger out of here." Ken stepped up to him, inquiring, "Do you believe in Jesus?" taking on the task of attempting racial reconciliation with a casually encountered, armed posse.

This is an extraordinary amount of information for a first session, and important clues to Ken's core image patterns are laid out, at least in embryonic form, for the work that needs to be done in his movement toward wholeness and grounding.

Stress reduction methods are an immediate need, of course, but the long-term work concerns those many reported stories and memories of his childhood which have formed his patterns of behavior. It will require a combination of behavior modification and depth work. As the first level of work proceeds, the therapist listens carefully for the core patterns.

From the first session's stories, the therapist can see that Ken is a rescuer. Even stronger, he saw himself early on as the savior of his family, especially his mother. At the same time, in order to achieve his attempts to comfort and reconcile everyone, he offers himself as the sacrificial victim. From the birth story on, he will be sacrificed if others can thus be saved. He has managed to repress any feeling of personal hurt at his father's choice to sacrifice him at birth, has taken on the comforting of his mother for her loss of a child, has tried to repress his feelings of hurt when his sister derided him. Yet in later life any pain of another is felt by him as his personal pain—his "worst" pain. It is as if he can no longer suppress the level of pain his own sacrificial action causes him.

It should come as no surprise that Ken decided to become a

priest at the age of thirteen, entering into his studies to prepare. That training reinforced his learning to give himself away, but the only receiving he did was with God. He came to know a close relationship with God; he said he knew "God would hold onto me." This sense of a close personal, caring relationship with God helped him through his early years of priesthood.

At the beginning of his therapy, Ken turned his attention to his own feelings, trying to perceive his own responses, beyond his mask of how he thought he "should" feel. He saw that any little thing could tick him off and that he was full of unexpressed anger. Yet at the same time, he could be drained by any needy person or hurting person he was around. He had difficulty *not* responding to every need, but then felt done in, driven, even short of breath.

He realized that he lived by an unstated rule or "injunction," as he called it: to please others first, even to his own harm. As he tried to give himself permission to give up that rule of life, he remembered asking as a child, "Why do I always have to give up?" The pattern was sometimes so strong in him that he even faced within himself a desire to die in order to get out of the level of pain he lived with. He said the realization that he could stop this pattern felt like "the beginning of the rest of my life."

Yet he had so few boundaries between himself and other people that it was almost as if he had no skin, being just open to all the influences of other people whom he met, even peripherally. When he was caught in the pattern of trying to meet all the needs of all comers, he was reminded of a repetitive childhood dream which came during a high fever.

He dreamed that he was on a train on a railroad track which went in a circle. The train began to move and then just went faster and faster until he would scream and wake. The dream expressed how he felt when he used himself up for others, and he needed to wake up to that fact in outer life.

The healing image that came to him after all these realizations was that he needed to learn to hold his ground whenever he felt the need to justify himself, either to himself or others, instead of giving up his ground in sacrificial acts. His trying to please had the shadow purpose of making him feel acceptable, which he only felt himself to be when he was performing right. It was like a return of his old scrupulosity, with the force of a condemning, internalized pope and college of cardinals—all pointing blaming fingers at him. Yet it was he himself who laid the unrealistic requirements on himself. So his motto when he caught himself in this pattern became Hold Your Ground.

He reported experiencing a "continual frenzy to fix things," and also of doing it manipulatively. This came about after he began to make boundaries between himself and other people. He experienced trying to resist handing over more and more of himself to his family or to his church, but feeling always a terrible pull to do so. When he was at this point, he was really seeing his old destructive pattern and holding his ground against it.

He was encountering not only his own family pattern—the role he was chosen to fill for his family of origin, but something in the Christian religious pattern as well. So his "family pattern" refers not only to his own family of origin, but also to his "religious family" pattern.

There is a central cultural vision of the Western Christian world of self-sacrifice, patterned on the sacrifice of Jesus and the Christian martyrs. It is part of the reason that many religious people object to the inner work of self-knowledge, in the mistaken notion that one cannot be truly Christian if one focuses "too much" on oneself—whatever that means.

Many people, as with Ken, try hard all their lives to live with truly self-destructive behaviors in the name of Christian self-sacrifice, but we will not tolerate our own self-annihilation. It is a travesty of Jesus' sacrifice on the cross to equate it with the destruction of part of God's creation—the human creation. Somehow, within the ethical and moral limits of the Western world, we must find an appropriate way of living which is neither the selfish disregard of others nor the destruction of ourselves.

This kind of unqualified self-sacrifice is challenged by many feminist theologians, in an attempt to help women recover from the cultural messages they have been given. Don Browning also suggests a reconciling vision, when he urges that mutuality or equal regard for all people is a deep goal of the Christian life, though in "this sinful and broken world we have to sacrifice ourselves and work actively and sometimes endure pain in an attempt to restore mutuality."[4] Sacrifice is thus put in its place, not as the goal itself, but sometimes as an appropriate means to the true goal.

In this view, self-sacrifice and suffering are a transitional ethic, not the main goal, which is mutuality of persons and equal regard. As Ken works to get beyond his family's acceptance of his willing sacrifice which he began as a tiny boy, he must work through his own theology of sacrifice toward accepting himself as a person who can serve, but still hold his ground.

Bloody Jesus Died on the Cross

The shocking title of this example comes straight from the core image of a woman who called herself "a recovering Catholic." From her early church training, Diane, as I will call her, deeply internalized a personal guilt which, as an adult in her thirties, she described like this: "Bloody Jesus died on the cross, and it's all my fault." Having taken in this guilt, she spent her youth trying to atone for her guilt with increasingly stringent penances, but she never felt free of it. Penance for her, instead of being a way of being freed from guilt, became a cycle of holding on to it.

At the same time, as a devout little girl, she felt surrounded by angels ("I always hung out with the angels") and she always loved God passionately. Trying to make sense of her own experience and the teaching of the Catholic church as best she could understand it, willing to follow her catechism, she reasoned with her child's reasoning in a manner which carried out her love of God and her family dynamics around her felt passion as well. Since she loved God, she felt she needed to punish herself to show her love. She would say in prayer, "OK, God, if you want me to do this, if it pleases you, I'll do it passionately with all my being. I'll bloody myself in penance."

As she grew up and her body changed, she connected her "sin" with any feelings of sexuality she felt. This seemed in conflict with "God," since sexuality had been taught her as having to do with her sinful body, and so she considered this further evidence of her depravity.

Her family situation, in a strict, patriarchal family system, exacerabated this very early. She was the eldest child, but her brother was born only a year after she was. An early traumatic memory concerned her throwing a bottle at her little brother and gashing his head, expressing outwardly the natural hostility she felt in the competition for love. Families are frequently horrified at the vigor of sibling attacks, but it is my observation that the only reason small children don't destroy each other is that they lack the manual dexterity.

Diane related incidents where she evidently tried to get beyond her view of Christianity-as-guilt. One Easter, she "heard" the mass as a ritual of unconditional love, compassion, innate harmony, and healing presence. As with most attempts to share a religious experience, however, hers sounded "stupid" to her when she thought of sharing it with her family, and she retreated back into her old negative pattern: maybe if I suffer enough, I'll be rescued.

As in the example of Ken above, though, Diane's self-abnegation was not possible without a heavy price. The family configuration, cultural views of the role of women, as well as the church patterns made her connect this guilt-penance pattern with gender. The priests and Jesus were all men, and it was they whom she experienced as laying the guilt on her. Her own displacement by her baby brother added to this, as did her mother's "man-hating stuff."

Her father's treatment of her added an odd aspect. He protected her so much that she was never given responsibility, and she ended up thinking herself helpless. She fancied that he thought her incapable of responsible action and felt that she had to be perfect to be acceptable. She couldn't achieve perfection, of course, so she felt guilty about her very personhood. As an adult, in therapy, she said the idea of having *choices* in life was completely new to her; she was still something like a helpless child in her own view.

It is not surprising that she married her husband in the hope that his caring for her could somehow free her from her entrapment in guilt and penance, but no one else can free us as long as we ourselves are caught in these old negative merry-go-rounds.

Yet something in her rebelled at this constant guilt and penance. She tried to get free of it by leaving the church, but it was too deeply embedded in her personal patterns for this to achieve her freedom from guilt. It helped in some ways by relieving the constant reinforcement of the "bloody" pattern, but one result was that she simply lost any regular place to be in contact with her religious experiences.

Children make sense of life as best they can with the material they have available. As more positive ways were closed off, Diane turned to some very negative ones. If she was to be kept a child, she turned into a very bratty one. When her emotions would well up, she would get enraged when she didn't get her own way, like a small child. As long as the rage was suppressed, it came out only passively-aggressively and in depression. As she began to let the rage into consciousness, she realized that she wanted vengeance, especially (she began to see) against men.

She would then remember what she felt she had been taught: that anger was a sin, so she would turn the rage against herself, begin to "trash" herself, and be off again on the old pattern of "crucifying" herself with penances to make up for how terrible she was. Ritually, she was stuck at Good Friday.

On an even deeper level, we could say that Diane took on to herself an inflation, by identifying with Jesus Christ. She was unable when it got that deep to distinguish between herself and the archetype of the savior; she was both victim and victimizer and thus "had" to sacrifice herself.

As she began symbolic work with this core image, Diane had several interesting dreams with clarifying motifs. In one dream, she and a nurse friend (a healing shadow figure) were traveling to Italy (connected with Roman Catholicism?) and had with them a dictionary to "know what the words meant." It's as if the dream suggests she needs a bigger picture of God than the one she has from childhood—a dictionary to look up meanings.

One dream showed her waiting for a ritual so she could make an offering, and the theme of a healing ritual became a central one for her. The same night another dream showed her with a new house and waking up—two themes of change.

Another dream a few weeks later portrayed her as docile, innocent, and naive. When she behaved in that manner—docile, innocent, and naive—the dream imagery said she was "married" to a cruel doctor (an OB-GYN) who hates women. This dream highlights the patterns mentioned above and shows how the docile Diane is "married" to (that is, dependent on, tied to) the cruel inner figure who hates and wounds her. When she behaves in a docile manner, it brings out within her a compensatory cruelty toward herself—and then she "trashes" herself. She cannot deny her true self with impunity.

Diane began to see that she had spent her life waiting for life to come to her, with no idea of herself as having power over her own life. Yet as she tried to make changes in her own behavior patterns, seeing her own self-sabotage and perfectionism, she felt thwarted by all her old self-messages and commented, "This waking up stuff is *hard.*"

After several months of continuing this hard work, a ritual came from deep within herself. She had been in search of healing in a number of places, including an energizing women's support group which worked with music and other aspects of women's spirituality. These rituals were life affirming for her, free of guilt, penance, and performance. She experienced in one such Easter ritual a strong presence of unconditional love of all that is, personified in the healing presence of the resurrected, archetypal Jesus Christ.

Then one night when she had some time alone without husband or children, a ritual rose from her core. As she followed her own intuitions from minute to minute, it was as if she danced out and wove together many previously conflicting aspects. Without invading her own actions, let me say that she felt she danced through the bloody Jesus of Good Friday to his resurrection at Easter and through a spectrum of feminine symbols and nature cycles from winter to spring. She was empowered by getting in touch with her rage, which energized her ritual, helping her turn a corner and have the choice to transform the power of dark rage into light and life and rebirth. Even, in the most powerful imagery of all, the menstrual blood "uncleanness" of women was transformed into the deep feminine potential for birth, juxtaposed with a sense of her blood guilt and penance for the "bloody Jesus" being cleansed and washed away. She said it ended in quiet waiting and genuine humility, like a seed, waiting for God to quicken—a creative ritual combining masculine and feminine. She felt held in unconditional love and wholeness.

In the weeks that followed, Diane certainly did not experience any magical changes. The hard work was still to do, day by day, but she had a real sense of having turned a corner. At work, she felt in charge and responsible. Coincidentally, her husband was in a rough time at his office, and she was able to offer him comfort in his need. She was conscious of separating out evil from mere unconsciousness, so that power and its use could be truly seen as an ethical and moral issue.

She then had a dream in which a spider jumped on her neck as she tried to protect her little boy. It felt to her like a negative feminine image of her guilt—one which she had to work to differentiate. It is very hard to be a good mother when one has not been appropriately mothered oneself, and Diane had a lot of work to do. She was still in search of a supportive community in which this work could continue, and the healthy part of the traditions lived through to be freed from the negative core image. The image itself, of course, as she becomes more awake, points to its healing. As her own ritual showed her, she can move from Good Friday to Easter.

She had given men all her power, including the men in the church as well as men in her family and her boyfriends; then she had been consumed with the desire for vengeance against them for taking her power away and leaving her guilty. She deeply wished to change this pattern, and, as if in support of her desire, she dreamed that her father had died (her symbolic inner tyrant father), and she woke the next morning feeling loved and secure.

Those core images incurred in our families and other systems are some of the most difficult to free ourselves from. The popularity of the inner child work of John Bradshaw and others attests to the common human experience of being caught in received patterns which need to be healed so that we can move on.

Bradshaw urges that we learn to feel our pain from childhood and begin to nurture ourselves, accepting that we were wounded and need healing. Hugh Missildine points out that we tend, as we grow up, to internalize the way we feel ourselves to be treated by our parents and then begin to treat ourselves the same way.[5] Alice Miller's work has had enormous influence in helping people realize that families which looked quite "normal" have nonetheless left many without any adequate sense of themselves.[6] Heinz Kohut encourages therapists to reflect people back to themselves in an empathic attempt to heal such early wounds to the sense of self.[7] In family reconstruction experiences, groups help each other re-experience and reconfigure the way in which families tend to contaminate the past with the present, so that new learning becomes possible.[8]

All these and many others, especially the family systems theorists, have given us ways to work with healing, and any counselor will affirm their usefulness. In the midst of it all, the concept of listening for the core images and then using them to point the way toward healing is a helpful adjunct. We then deal not just with the specific harm done, as such, but also with the larger symbolic meaning which the core image carries and the future healing possibilities to which it points.

·4·

Stories and Songs

Yeats wrote that there is "one myth" for every person, which if we knew it would make us understand all that the person did and thought.[1] Using "myth" in the same sense, Jung called the search for one's myth the "task of tasks."[2] When these men talk about myth, they are talking about the stories or dramas that reveal to us the way in which we are living our lives and our view of the world. They refer to stories that reveal patterns of what it means to be human.

When we connect at some level within ourselves with these timeless stories or dramas, we are in the patterns. We may be in different patterns at different times in our lives, and some of the myths may carry through far beyond their developmental moment. Myth in this sense of personal meaning includes both those important myths which speak to a culture or nation to which we belong and the smaller stories which speak to us as individuals about our lives. The search for our core images can include finding those stories which make us understand ourselves in the way Yeats meant.

In fact, Rollo May argues that contemporary therapy is "almost entirely concerned, when all is surveyed, with the problem of the individual's search for myths." He argues, along with many others in different fields, that the loss of myths in Western society is the direct cause of many of our problems and confusion. "Myths," he says, "are our self-interpretation of our inner selves in relation to the outside world." He further emphasizes this centrality of myth for psychotherapy:

Every individual who needs to bring order and coherence into the streams of her or his sensations, emotions, and ideas entering consciousness from within and without is forced to do deliberately for himself what in previous ages had been done for him by family, custom, church, and state. In the therapy myths may be a reaching out, a way of trying out new structures of life, or a desperate venture at rebuilding his or her broken way of life.[3]

Not only the "important" myths of cultures can serve this role for us. Even fictional stories that we remember well from childhood can be this kind of reaching out for coherence, and thus are clues to some of our core images, with the resulting aid in helping us discover patterns of behavior and belief and response. We wrote about such childhood stories at the beginning of *The Hero Journey in Dreams*.[4] I will review some of what we said there and then add to it the additional focus of core image work.

The first time I heard a lecturer speak on the subject of the importance of finding the myths and stories one lived by, the example given was of a woman who discovered one day that she was living her life under the story of the "Little Red Hen." That well-known children's story tells of a little red hen who found some seed one day in the barnyard and called out to the other barnyard animals to help her plant the seed. They all made excuses instead of coming to help her, and the little red hen said, "Well, I will then."

The story continues in the repetitive pattern of so many children's stories, as the little red hen asks for help at each stage—to water, weed, harvest, grind, and finally, to bake the bread. At each stage, all the other animals declare themselves unable to help her, and she says, "Well, I will then."

Then, when bread-eating time comes, all the animals volunteer to help her. In one version of the story which our children read, the end of the story was "cleaned up," and the little red hen shared the bread with everyone. The original version of the story, however, has the little red hen reply, "No, I planted it, I watered it, I weeded it, I harvested it, I ground it, I baked it, and now I am going to eat it." The last paragraph of the book says, "And she did."

This story is a good illustration of the way one "lives" a well-known story. The woman who "lived" the story of the little red hen discovered that her patterns of behavior typically matched those in the story. When she asked for help in any area (or even when there was just a task that needed to be done, say, in the family or office), she accepted the excuses given by others with a sweet little smile—and did the task alone.

What the story suggests, of course, is that resentment builds up in the little red hen (even if the little red hen is unconscious of the resentment), and someday she will rebel. Once this woman realized that she was continually acting out the story of the little red hen, she could afterward identify her own typical behavior in each individual instance. She had found a core image of her life.

What does she do with the information? That decision is hers; she may even make different decisions in different situations, of course. At one time, she may decide that she would rather go ahead and *be* a little red hen, because the matter is not important enough to make an issue of. Another time she may decide: enough is enough. Whatever she decides in each instance, she is making a more informed decision, with a much clearer awareness of the possible consequences of each choice, all based on the understanding of a core image of how she tends to function. The person who becomes aware of such patterns in herself or himself is able to function in a more balanced and healthy way. The pattern is less likely to be controlling.

After this lecture on the little red hen, I began to search for my own myths or stories. The first storybook character I identified in my behavior patterns was a character called the "little toy clown" in the children's book *The Little Engine That Could*.

In that story, the engine breaks down on a train carrying dolls and toys for children. All the dolls and toys begin to cry because the children won't have any dolls and toys to play with, but the little toy clown jumps up and calls for everyone to cheer up—their engine isn't the only engine in the world and surely someone else will help them. Then follow several scenes where the little toy clown flags down other engines and presents the problem to them, only to be knocked rudely aside. Each time the dolls and toys begin to cry, and each time the little toy clown repeats his theology of hope, backed up with the action of flagging down more engines.

Finally, a very little engine offers to help them and struggles up the mountain with the now famous line, "I think I can. I think I can," which, after successfully negotiating the top, changes to the triumphant, "I thought I could. I thought I could."

That story was balanced later by my finding another story that I lived by: Chicken Little. A nut falls on Chicken Little one day, at which she immediately decides, "The sky is falling!" She runs to find the wise Owl to give her advice. On the way, she runs into several other barnyard birds, who ask her (sensibly) how she knows the sky is falling in. She always replies (not quite truthfully), "I saw it with my eyes. I heard it with my ears. Some of it fell on my tail."

All the other birds join her until the whole crowd reaches the Owl, who says (skeptically requiring more than hearsay evidence), "Let me see the sky that fell on you. Then I will tell you what to do." Chicken Little leads them back to the place where she was when the panic hit. After looking everywhere around, they find the nut, at which the Owl laughs and says, "You want me to tell you what to do. Laugh, Chicken Little, and we will too."

Chicken Little, probably an extravert intuitive personality type like me, panics and *thinks* she has perceived the end of the world with her sensate functions of seeing and hearing. In fact, of course, her very panic prevents her from using these less well developed functions until she gets some help from her friend the Owl, this folk tale's wisdom figure.

Reflecting on stories that were important to us as children can thus be a good source of finding core image patterns, with their continuing perspective on our responses to life situations. We have frequently kept just that book or perhaps tried to interest our own children in our favorites. In my own case, I had bought my children *The Little Engine That Could* as one of their earliest books. Further, when I moved the last trunks away from my parents' attic, I found my first reader. The first story in it was Chicken Little, and my childish crayon drawings are up and down the margins of each page of that one story.

After a workshop on childhood stories, a man offered another good example. He said that the minute he heard the suggestion of reflecting on a childhood story which resonated with how one lived one's life, he thought of Humpty Dumpty. "Humpty Dumpty sat on a wall. Humpty Dumpty had a great fall. All the king's horses

and all the king's men couldn't put Humpty Dumpty together
again." He realized that he was terribly afraid of failure in all of
his life—as if, if he "fell," he'd never be put back together again.

A woman told of connecting herself with the story of the ugly
duckling. She evidently was a kind of ugly little girl, and her grandfather even called her his duckling. She felt her healing when, as an
older person, she looked at herself in the mirror and with pleasure
found herself thinking, "You know, you're not so bad looking."
She had let herself become a swan.

Clarinda

I was given a good example after a workshop of how a beloved
early childhood story can be used by a child, yet understood in a
completely different way as an adult. This illustrates how the core
image can point the way beyond its early effect on us toward a
mature adult pattern.

This story was told by a woman who attended the workshop
and later got in touch with me to describe what she learned. She
said the story she wrote about in the workshop reflection time was
her favorite one as a girl. She had recently moved across the country
to get married, and she even brought this child's book with her
(the only one she brought of all her children's books). I'll quote
her own words and then comment on the image of her story.

> *Clarinda* was the book that I loved as a little girl and remem-
> bered through my adulthood. And the thing I remembered about
> it was that she always had an escape route from her home be-
> cause when she got angry and things weren't going well, she
> could get in the bathtub and pull the plug and go down the drain
> and out the spout and into this little pond and play with the
> ducks and the foxes and the turtles. And it was a *wonderful* kind
> of fantasy for me of being able to go deep down inside into my
> imagination and escape from the difficulties of my family life.

Let me interrupt her story to make clear that what I have just
quoted was in essence what she wrote in the workshop. Then after
the workshop she went home and read the book again, and the
following is the additional information she told me about what she

learned by contrasting her memory of the story and the story as she encountered it when she reread it.

> And when I went back to read the story after our workshop together and read the chapters, I realized that really what was happening and what I had forgotten was that everytime Clarinda went down to play, she would learn a moral lesson that taught her to come back to her home and do exactly what her parents had told her to do.
>
> So there was one example where she was throwing a tantrum because she didn't want to wear her petticoats and she didn't want to wear her white socks and she didn't want to wear her maryjanes. So she went down and down and down and came out to play. And she learned there that that kind of behavior— she learned it from something that the ducks did [here I noticed on the recording she left for me that her whole voice became tired-sounding as she described the moral lesson to be learned]— that that kind of behavior was not appropriate. So when she went back to her house, she smilingly and sweetly put on her petticoats and her white socks and her maryjanes.
>
> And the startling thing to me was that what I remembered was the escape while what is true in my family life was I always complied. I rebelled inside, but I always complied with a sweet smile. And that story is more my life than I had ever realized. So if you can use it, good.

She was comforted as a child by the story and the idea that one could escape into imagination. The story thus helped her to survive. Yet it also showed her as a reflective adult the ways in which the pattern of complying had operated on her even out of her favorite escape literature. She described feeling a sense of awe at this discovery about herself. Though I don't know more of her story, I would make a "clinical" bet that she has had to work through this same disjunction in her theology and her relation to God.

As such stories are worked with, their very dissonances become significant in understanding how the core images they act out influence our lives. Bruno Bettelheim tells a story of a woman in a fairy-tale workshop who was angry at the way fairy tales always emphasized males as heroic and portrayed females as passive and in need of being rescued.

Her example was Hansel and Gretel, which she claimed to remember vividly; and she railed against the portrayal of Gretel as passive and in need of being rescued by Hansel. Bettelheim suggested she reread the story, and of course she had it backwards. Hansel is the one who is imprisoned, being fattened up by the witch, while Gretel is made to work. It is in fact Gretel who kills the witch and rescues Hansel.[5] He said in a talk that the woman was so sure of her memory that she did a lot of research, looking for the *real* story she was certain she had read as a child.

Bettelheim points out facts in her own life which reinforced the way she remembered Hansel and Gretel. You could say that the way she remembered the story, though not the *real* story, was her real core image. As with the woman who loved *Clarinda*, her own early experience confirmed the "false" story, but the "true" story can be used by the adult to change her patterns. The story which had enraged her for its "male chauvinism" could point the way toward her own overcoming and redemption.

The Goat and the Train

Songs can also contain our core images; they may even stay with us in a special way because they have not only their story line, but the musical accompaniment as well. For a similar reason, there is probably more popular theology taught in hymns than in all the scripture classes a church has; Charles Wesley probably has taught more people than his brother John, even with John's reputed thirty thousand sermons. Sometimes core images can connect even from TV jingles or equally trivial sources. All of us know the experience of getting a tune on our mind and being unable to escape from it. When they last a whole lifetime, they may contain core images.

A young minister, whom I will call Steve, discovered two such songs from his childhood which wove themselves into a complicated tapestry through his life. These two songs and their themes are core images of his. The first of them which he identified in his personal search was a folk song called "Bill Grogan's Goat," which he had learned to play on the piano in John Thompson's Second Grade Book.[6] His process of discovery, beginning with this folk song, demonstrates the labyrinthine task of tracing core images in our lives. Incidentally, because of this complex interweaving, this example could equally well appear in any of the other chapters—

memories, family history, or dreams. His core images are in all of them.

Steve had taken a dream to a group for interpretive work. In the dream the leader of a group was trying to make Steve do things at which he balked. He described the leader as "a slightly built, bearded Pan-like male." This leader told Steve that he (Steve) "was acting like an animal" because he wouldn't submit; then warned he would have to leave the group if he continued to refuse.

He had dreamed the dream several years before at a time when he was interviewing for the job he now held as an associate pastor at a church. He thought of it at this particular life juncture because two men in the congregation had told him he must stop using inclusive language "or else." Their warning had evoked his old dream for him. It was the same pattern of being told that there was something wrong with him and unless he straightened up and submitted to authority, he would be forced to leave.

As he worked with the dream in the group, he realized that the feeling was a very familiar one for him through his whole life. He had always felt "wrong" in his family, and that was repeatedly affirmed for him by events and his family's messages to him. His life frequently seemed to be on the line; he lived on the edge.

His mother almost miscarried him on Christmas Eve before he was born the following June. When he was two, his mother fell over him, broke her leg, and (he discovered years later) miscarried. It was always referred to in the family as the time Steve broke mom's leg. His sense of his life was that he went from one disaster to another, and this carried over into adult life. Once after he visited his family of origin, his mother sent him a cartoon of Dagwood goofing up, with the clear intent to compare Steve to Dagwood.

In addition, in his associations with the dream imagery, Steve described Pan as "half-goat, half-man." Then he added that the message he got from his family was that he had to be the family goat, and he said, "I do it!" It was at this point that, somehow, "Bill Grogan's Goat" came up.

A member of the group (along with Steve) had learned to play the piece on the piano as a youngster, and remembered the words:

> Bill Grogan's goat was feeling fine,
> Ate three red shirts from off the line;

Bill took a stick, gave him a whack,
And tied him to the railroad track.

The whistle blew, the train drew nigh,
Bill Grogan's goat was doomed to die;
He gave three groans of awful pain,
Coughed up the shirts and flagged the train.

The group had a laugh over the song, but even then, at the beginning of the core image exploration, Steve sensed a serious note for him in the story. He had been beaten up on figuratively and left as if to die. Much later he realized that if Bill Grogan's goat had died on the track, everyone would have said the accident was the goat's fault; but, as with Steve in his family, it was neither an accident nor Steve's fault. He was the victim, who had managed to survive.

That was about the end of the discussion in the group, and Steve really forgot about the song and the dream and interpretation because he was so caught up in crisis in his outer life. He was in the job as associate pastor of the church for which he had been interviewing at the time of his original dream.

He was also in an exciting time in his life, where his own sense of how to carry out his vocation had been coming clearer to him. He had felt a call to emphasize the inner journey, what he called "a kind of call to go into spiritual direction." However, his own tradition does not use that language and offered no specialized vocation. He tried some meditation on his own, but was not successful. He decided to try pastoral psychotherapy as the nearest way he could think of to exercise this sense of vocation.

He was excited about sorting out how to be a parish pastor and a pastoral counselor, especially as a way of reclaiming the inner journey, which he felt his church had abandoned. He felt he was "coming into his own."

In the midst of this excitement, the problems had arisen with a part of the leadership of the rather conservative congregation where he was serving, in part because of his attempts to introduce these "new" ideas into his teaching and pastoral care work.

The congregation was split between those who liked the new ideas and those who did not, and the situation grew so bad that both he and the senior pastor were asked to leave as a resolution of the conflict. The senior pastor said no. Then a denominational leader said to Steve, "You're the only solution." The leader admitted that in many ways Steve was a victim in the situation, but he seemed to view that as inevitable, as if (sigh) though too bad, that's how it is.

He had been in counseling during this difficult period, and he had been well coached with family systems work on ways to deal with the church. He reported that in one of his last counseling sessions, his counselor was just totally exhausted and at a dead-end, a stalemate, and looked at Steve as if to say, "Why didn't it work? Everything we tried."

Steve said, "Something happened when he told me he couldn't help me. To me he is one of the best psychotherapists in town, and I had put a lot of faith in the intellect and its ability. When he said, 'I'm sorry. I can't help you,' I was on my own."

So Steve had accepted his severance, and he went out into unemployment. During this time he turned back to his earlier sense of vocation and took some courses in contemplative prayer, eventually joining the contemplative prayer staff as a secretary. He was sustained by this prayer and his part-time job.

About the same time, he was asked to preach for four weeks at a rural church, and he ended up serving as an interim pastor for a year. The living situation was far from ideal, and he was alone for extended periods of time; but the unheated cabin became his hermitage, and he later viewed the time as one of purification.

Several years later, in an interview about using this example as a core image for this book, Steve's insights had multiplied exponentially. For one thing, he had been watching the pattern of being the goat in his family. He began to listen to family interactions in his biological family with a tuned ear. He became aware that unconsciously, that's how his family was using him.

One time at a family party he had what seemed a paradigmatic experience. He was standing in the kitchen talking to his dad in an affectionate moment, talking about each other's early family life and being kids and having brothers and sisters. His sister, who was listening in, blurted out, "Well, you were a mistake from the beginning."

Steve had also reviewed some of the events of his severance with

his former church job. He remembered that when the denominational leader came to the meeting with the church elders at the
height of the conflict, his opening statement was, without even
hearing or knowing any of the facts, "Well, usually in situations
like this, the associate leaves."

Steve saw that the outcome of the church upheaval was a foregone
conclusion, despite any assurances the denominational leaders gave
him. He put it in terms of his core image: the associate role is a
goat role.

He reviewed another conversation he had with a denominational
executive before a special congregational meeting which had been
called after Steve's resignation was announced. Many people in the
congregation were upset because Steve was leaving, and they
wanted to know why. The executive came to Steve and said, "The
church is so in uproar, I'm afraid they'll tear the church to pieces.
I need you to stand up at the meeting. I'm appealing to you; you
don't have to do this, and I would understand if you say no. But
I'm appealing to you to be ready to stand up before the congregation and make a statement, because they don't know what's going
on. It's a closed, clergy system. For you to make a statement, that
will put as much of this to rest as possible."

Here is Steve's interview account of what happened:

> Well, the great day came. One side was here, and one was there.
> The microphone was here and there was anger. They didn't
> know what to say. Somebody said, "We want an explanation.
> We want to know what's going on." [The executive] looks at me
> and the pastor and asked if the pastors would come forward and
> shed some light. The senior pastor didn't make a move.
>
> So I got up. I knew my time had come. I just opened my
> heart and spoke. And I spoke impersonally. I spoke without
> saying it's this fault or that fault. I just said, this is the situation
> as I see it. I don't want to stay. I want to go. I spoke for three
> or four minutes. And I got a standing ovation, and I sat down
> and I was crying. It was really painful.

Steve was the hero in one sense, because he was cheered, but he
was also out of a job. When was he a goat? What could he do about
it? I mentioned that Steve later identified another core image song.
His additional work with this core image of the little goat tied to

the railroad (and with his second core image song) is such a good example of how to work with core images that I will summarize his further work in chapter 9, "Working Through Case Material," because it can serve as a model example of where such a core image can lead.

The Stubborn Little Burro

The next example was given me by someone who heard a presentation I gave on core images. She said as she sat in the audience listening, she found herself thinking of a book called *Brighty and the Grand Canyon*, and she wondered why.

It was so intriguing to her that she went home that evening and found it on a bookshelf in her basement. As best she could remember, she got it in third or fourth grade—"one of those where you can order books, and you get stars for how many books you read. And I probably—I'm a book collector anyway—and I probably had fifty to a hundred of these paperback books when I was younger. But I saved maybe three. But what was important was *Brighty and the Grand Canyon*."

She pulled the book out that night from her basement bookshelf and read on the back cover: "'You no-good beast,' the man shouts at Brighty. 'If I didn't need you for a guide, I'd feed you to the ravens.' Brighty, the wild burro was trapped by an escaping murderer. With a cruel whip, the man forces Brighty to lead him up the dangerous trail. 'If I can get across the state line, I'll be safe,' thinks the murderer. But Brighty is as stubborn as a burro can be, and more than anything he is determined to be free again."[7]

This last sentence was the most important to her and moved her strangely. What struck her then was how freedom has been a theme for her. As she retold the story in an interview, her voice was full of delight in this child's story:

> The story of Brighty and the Grand Canyon is about this burro that is this free spirit and loving and is known by all the miners in the area for his mischievousness and his ability to enjoy the canyon, and he's just kind of this real loved burro that does good deeds and is this wonderful spirit. And then he gets captured by this murderer that's trying to get over the state line and is abused

in a number of different ways. Finally at the end, the bad guy has to pull the wagon that pulls the burro and this other guy out of where they are in the canyon, because Brighty is wounded. And it's like justice is done is what is profound to me in that, and this free spirited burro that gets captured and trapped—I don't know. It seems to be the story of my life in some ways.

In exploring the way in which this little burro was important for her, she reviewed how she had been "trapped within the memories as well as the emotional and physical abuse of my gang rape when I was twelve." The story was powerful to her "because he was able to have freedom and the bad guy got imprisoned and taken off and Brighty was the hero." She added, "So the core image for me is freedom and determination to be free, to live with a lightheartedness and a friskiness."

Not only had she experienced the gang rape she mentioned, but at five or six, she had been sexually molested by her brother and two friends. From that earlier experience she was left with a deep sense of shame by the comments of her mother and the boys' mother, who treated her as being to blame—an all too frequent occurrence in such cases. This was magnified at twelve by the gang rape of her and a girl friend of hers. The rapists shamed her as being inadequate, then tied her up and forced her to watch them rape her friend. She had subsequently been in therapy as an adult and experienced a lot of healing from these early traumas, but becoming aware that Brighty was a core image for her began to make other connections.

In continuing core image work, she made another association to an early childhood experience that was passed down through her mother. She asked her mother one day when she was three or four what her own name was, and when her mother, puzzled by the question, told her, she said, "But my sister called me Stupie." The story was told at major family events. It was one of those stories that would always get a good laugh, and she would laugh right along with everybody. However, she reports:

> I always kind of felt at a deeper level kind of hurt by that, because I always felt not very intelligent and kind of stupid. So through my growth process and the working on myself and I

think Myers-Briggs was one of the most beneficial in helping to see that my intellect is not through the T function, but that I'm such a strong F and N that it's just a different type of intelligence, and so I've worked through that.

But what I found to be really fascinating with all of this is last Christmas, Mama put a new light on this story that has been passed down for as long as I can remember. She put the story into context as to where the scene was played, which was at the neighborhood swimming pool. Why my sister called me Stupie was that I had jumped off the high diving board and I wasn't supposed to. And I mean that really says what kind of kid I was. It was like: if I want to do it, by God I was going to do it.

And my sister was in charge of me down there, and it made her real scared and upset, and she made me go home. And on the way home, she called me stupid because I wasn't supposed to do that—which really is interesting to me in terms, first of all, of not knowing the whole story of why she would call me stupid, and how that had had an effect, but the whole story gives me a whole different image of myself.

I was a gutsy kid. I did stuff I wanted to do. I went out on the ledge, you know, which also comes back to Brighty and the Grand Canyon. I mean, he was a little burro that did whatever he wanted to and enjoyed life.

Brighty, which she loaned me to read, is the story of a wild burro who has been named after Bright Angel Creek by some men he has befriended in the Grand Canyon. Sometimes Brighty lets children ride him and carries water for his friends, but never lets adults ride or others force him to carry things. As one friend says, "Who kin rope a wild, free spirit?" (p. 83)

Brighty has repeated adventures, always with the focus on his being a free spirit. This is true even one summer when President Theodore Roosevelt and his son come for a lion hunt, and the president tells of his dream of making the Grand Canyon a national park. Brighty even takes part in the dedication of the bridge over the Colorado River by President Roosevelt.

An afterward in the book talks of people still telling the story of Brighty, who made the trail to the North Rim, "the roving spirit of the Grand Canyon—forever wild, forever free" (p. 223).

It seems clear that this little free-spirited girl made a connection with the little free-spirited burro in the book, and the character in the book helped her stubbornly to resist shame and to learn to know herself to be something of a hero. Both the experience of being sexually molested and the experience of being called stupid contained strong pulls toward shame. In fact, the sexual molestation probably affirmed her "stupid" name in the child's mind.

One writer on childhood abuse uses a strangely appropriate image to describe such feelings:

> With such overwhelming messages from both family and society, many [childhood abuse] survivors internalize the belief that they are damaged and unworthy human beings. After all, if enough people call you a jackass, you might just go out and buy yourself a saddle.[8]

Instead of "buying a saddle," this survivor found a burro-hero to identify with—stubborn, free spirited, forever wild and free. The delight that the grown woman still took in the childhood character is the kind of delight the image helped her learn to take in herself.

A Motherless Child

A recording by Peter, Paul, and Mary unexpectedly broke Rebecca up into sobs one night when it came on the stereo. The song was "Sometimes I feel like a motherless child." Rebecca had grown up like many in middle America, thinking that she really came from a very nice family, though, of course, there were some problems, which she tended to minimize. She had gained a great deal of knowledge about herself, her sense of depression, and her relation with her family during her therapy, but even after a lot of understanding, hurts can still remain.

She had tried to talk about some of what she had learned with her mother, but her mother was not interested. She finally saw that her mother was a very unconscious person who chose to remain that way. Her mother, on the surface, was more than attentive to her, but Rebecca's most helpful breakthrough came after learning some of Kohut's theories about mirroring reflection. She came to see that, though her mother was apparently dedicated to her, she has *never* seen her. Further, her mother was really uninterested in what Rebecca achieved in life, the most frustrating part of that being that the mother would never recognize that fact.

She saw that her relation to her mother was certainly not as bad as many others, but there was, nonetheless, a lot of pain, in part because of what a child always wants from her mother. She came to the point where (when she was feeling centered and strong) she could just think that it was sad that her mother didn't get the daughter she would have liked and Rebecca herself didn't get the mother she would have liked.

She learned to protect herself from her mother by setting up strong boundaries (which her mother would never do, so she did it alone). She tried to fulfill what she saw as her Christian duty to honor her mother just because she was her mother. She realized, "I do love part of her, in that she does many generous things and had herself a rather hard life. I honor her for giving me life and doing all the difficult things that parents have to do for children to survive. She never beat me nor colluded in some of the terrible incest stories that many people have experienced."

All that was when she felt strong and centered. When she was not strong and centered, of course, her mother's slightest comment could send her into paroxysms of guilt and anger. But, she said, "I know it now, so I can eventually get out of it, back to where I depend on her for nothing."

The song which had moved her to tears was ultimately a big help to her, because of its words. It goes: "Sometimes I feel like a motherless child [repeated three times] a long way from home." She used this as a pointer to see the direction she needed to go. She needed to find a home, which she felt such a long way from. *Home* was the healing symbol to which the song pointed. She couldn't get another mother; she could only have the one she was dealt. Home would never truly be with her mother, but must be whatever home she could find for herself. Home could be several things— with her husband, with her children and their families, with her religious community. Coming home also included working to be her true self—no longer falsified by either unthinking identification with her mother or unremitting anger at the loss of the ideal, affirming mother she longed for.

More than these, really, were her "unseen" homes. Her relation with God, though it continued to go through rough times and many changes, was her primary home. Her spiritual life—getting to that place of centeredness from which her strength came—was the way of staying in that home. Thus she made peace with her mother, her life, and her self through that image of the motherless child finding a home. She had discovered that her own recovery could not be limited by other people. Rebecca had to carry all the consciousness for her and her mother, because her mother would not, but she did not have to be tied up by anyone else's refusal or inability. Even a motherless child a long way from home could find her own home.

As with all core images, such stories and songs carry positive healing potential and thus become a powerful therapeutic growth tool. The stories and songs are myriad and can themselves point the way to their healing. They also have a particular effectiveness because they can be told and sung, with their levels of meaning increasingly apparent. It's as if each retelling of the story or singing of the song reinforces the way out. Almost more than any other core image source, the images from stories and songs seem to delight the people who have seen their personal significance. Each time brings a new healing.

·5·

Dreams

*D*ream images are one of the best ways to find core images; you might say they are the royal road to core images. This is true both of the lifelong images and of those which operate for a briefer time.

In working symbolically with core images that come from dreams, I think a special caution is in order. Because of some tendencies to view dream images in ways other than symbolic, it is even easier to get off the symbolic track. I have already suggested the danger of reifying images—at its most primitive level in the booklet from the grocery store check-out line.

Another is Freud's wish fulfillment theory of dream work, which I truly believe to have done incalculable harm to dream work. Jung absolutely rejected it, and he was right. It has, however, entered the collective consciousness of the twentieth century in an insidious way. The wish fulfillment theory of dream interpretation is not symbolic, but reductive—the antithesis of letting the dream images live on. It is based on the supposition that dreams are trying to conceal or hide information from us, rather than showing us some aspect of our lives of which we are not conscious.

If in fact the dreams are a natural, revelatory part of our psyche and its expression, then I think that interpreting all dreams as fulfilling the wishes of the dreamer has about as much validity as saying that if your nose itches, you're going to have a visitor. Yet we meet it everywhere we turn, once people know we know something about dreams.

Because there is difference of opinion about how to work with dreams, I will sketch briefly the method I am presupposing in work with dreams where core images appear. There are two main symbolic ways you can work with images. One primary way to work with images is interpretive—the organizing, structuring kinds of things. This is the thinking mode of analysis and differentiation. The other is imaginative, going back into it, dreaming it on, focusing, Gestalt techniques, active imagination, drawing the image, sculpting it, dancing it, acting it out, and those kinds of things—experiencing it or bringing it into our feeling life. I will mention some of these imaginative modes in more detail in chapter 8, "Treatment Planning."

Interpretation of Dreams

Wallace and I have outlined the main areas we think are important in dream-image interpretation in our first dream book, but I will mention them here briefly.

First, as Jung said, "Dreams are the natural reaction of the self-regulating psychic system,"[1] and the same thing can be said of core images wherever they come from. Our bodies have a self-regulating system—even if we hurt ourselves, say, with a cut. Certain actions can help the skin to heal, such as cleaning out the wound, stitching it together if it is serious, protecting it from additional wounding. But the body heals itself. We are so constructed that healing happens if nothing gets in its way.

Jung in effect suggests that the psyche also has this natural self-regulating system; it will heal itself if nothing gets in its way. Dreams are a part of this regulatory system, operating by a *compensatory* quality.

When one has an attitude or view which is too one-sided or exaggerated or even which is totally outside reality, the dream may show a picture of the opposite one-sided or exaggerated attitude. If the conscious ego is ignoring or unaware of some fact, the dream may hold it up to get our attention, as if to say, "Don't forget this part."

The second note of dream interpretation is the preference for working with a *series* of dreams, rather than simply isolated dreams. This can be especially helpful in core image work, because it is not uncommon for the same image or theme to appear more than once over a period of time. For one thing, if you miss the point of one dream, the dreams may well keep at you until you get it. As they do, the images may become darker and more troubled and even threatening. Seeing these changes in similar images is helpful to call attention to needed matters.

Even more important is the possibility of seeing patterns in a series of dreams, and this can happen particularly with important images which are at the core of the work. The same theme may be repeated, or a particular dream figure may recur repeatedly, but in slightly different situations. You may then discover implications or progression or development that you would not recognize in a single dream.

A third and crucial note of dream work is Jung's observation that the figures in dreams are sometimes to be interpreted *objectively* and sometimes *subjectively* (or sometimes both). When dream figures are interpreted objectively, they represent themselves, and the dream can be understood as concerning the dreamer's relationship with the dreamed-of person in outer life.

To look at a dream on the subjective level, you take each part of the dream as representing an aspect of yourself. You would then understand those dragons and rock stars and dictators and houses in your dream to be pointing to your inner dragons and rock stars and dictators and houses of your soul. Jung and most people who work with dreams find that most dreams are to be understood subjectively.

The fourth note of dream interpretation is Jung's brilliant and common-sense discovery of *amplification*. If you don't think the dream is trying to hide something from you (as Freud thought), but that it is trying to reveal something to you (as Jung thought), then the common-sense way to approach the picture language of the dream is to think what each person and image in the dream means to the dreamer.

Amplification includes any association—thoughts, feelings, sensations, intuitions, memories of any kind. Then, mysteriously, associations of other people can be offered to see if they help unravel the dream image. We can dream images which are illuminated by information from the whole history of human experience—from religion, mythology, history, folklore, anthropology, zoology, literature, fairy tales.

Finding Core Images in Dreams

So much for the general notes of symbolic work with dreams; now to focus on how the important core images can be identified. I have already suggested the most important clue: the feeling of the dreamer.

Another important clue can be the timing of the dream. The first dream one remembers is important, as are dreams on important anniversaries or birthdays. A dream remembered by an adult all the way from childhood can be especially significant. The initial dream is important. This may be a dream which comes just before dream work starts, or after the decision to start, or just after a first appointment with a therapist or spiritual director or after the first telephone contact.

If a core image seems to be in the initial dream, it is a continuing resource for the therapist or spiritual director as the work continues, or for inner work on your own. You can go back periodically and reread the initial dream, particularly if feeling confused about the work, to see if the dream becomes more clear in the light of later work and information. The initial dream may hold out the hope for a dreamer who feels hopeless, or it may give a warning which you need to stay aware of as the work proceeds.

Whether the clue to the core image is discovered from the feeling of the dreamer or from the timing of the dream, it is one which grabs the dreamer's attention and seems to resonate with some mysterious suggestion, or holding out hope or pointing toward a path. It seems to have motifs or themes about the life of the dreamer.

St. Monnica's Dream

A classic example (coming from the fourth century of our era) of a core image which was important for the life of the dreamer and her son was a dream which St. Augustine reports in his *Confessions*. Augustine's mother, Monnica, was an ardent Christian. Her oldest son Augustine was educated as a Christian; but he abandoned what little Christianity he had, became fascinated by the Manichean religion, and allied himself with it, to his mother's great distress. She never stopped praying for his conversion and seems never to have stopped following him around from city to city. A very determined lady, even though she followed him, she refused him her house and table, while weeping at her prayers, because, her son reports, "she so loathed the blasphemy and error in which I was swimming."[2]

About this time, Monnica had a dream which Augustine tells:

> In her dream she saw herself standing on a kind of measuring rule or wooden yardstick, wailing and overcome with grief. A radiant young man approached her in a happy and laughing mood and asked her the reason for this protracted weeping. (His purpose was not to learn from her but to teach her, as is customary in such dreams.) She replied that she was mourning the ruin of my soul. He then admonished her and, in a reassuring way, ordered her to look more carefully and she would see that I was standing next to her on the same measuring rule.[3]

She evidently immediately readmitted Augustine to her home and table and told him the dream. He disparaged the dream and told her it probably meant she would become a Manichean too. He was impressed, however, by her calm rejection of this interpretation because of the details of the dream. She told him the dream didn't say she would stand where he was, but that he would stand where she was. He says that for the nine remaining years of his "false darkness" she was sustained by the consolation of her dream.

I think it's fair to call this a core image for those years in Monnica's life. It gave her hope for the future and changed her behavior immediately. Her serenity in the face of his disparagement speaks of the strong feeling she had about the visitation of the radiant young man.

I am also intrigued by Augustine's interjected comment on the interpretation of her dream, which shows him accepting the natural, self-amplifying quality of her dream.

The Fighting Snakes

A comforting dream also came to a young woman I will call Cathy. She became engaged with all the excitement that surrounds that—getting her ring and beginning to plan the blending of their lives—and then in the same month her fiancé suddenly died. She sank into a black depression despite the support of friends and family. Shortly after seeking some counseling help with her grief, she dreamed this remarkable dream:

> In my dream there were two snakes fighting. One was much larger than the other. It was black and very gelid-looking. Almost non-skeletal. It was thick and long and seemed to quiver. The other was much smaller, wiry. It didn't have a color I remember.
>
> The serpents were fighting furiously. Striking, striking again and again at each other. While my face itself was not in the picture, I was in the background urging the smaller snake on. The little one had the identity of my younger sister Mary. It fought as though it were trying to protect me. She seemed so small in the face of the large black serpent, yet she was fighting so courageously and fiercely that I got the impression she might win. I awoke before the battle was concluded, but I felt that the battle had not been lost. In other words, I did not awake depressed, only with the awareness of this vivid, horrifying image.

This is a good example of the way in which dream images can communicate to the dreamer at a powerful level, even in the midst of the worst tragedies of life. Cathy knew all the words about loss and grief, and she was not without help, but none of them had the power to lift her black depression. This dream spoke to her core and helped her know at a deeply felt level that the power to overcome her grief was within her.

The most important personal associations needed to understand the dream were Cathy's descriptions of Mary. She described Mary as a "beautiful person, one who just lopes along and gets things done, someone everyone just loves." Her face lit up as she described some of the funny escapades and yet underlying responsibility which were parts of her sister Mary.

When Cathy was told that the dream images were parts of herself, she could see the black snake as a vivid picture of how her icy cold depression felt, but she could also see the courageous fight that the Mary-snake was putting up, urged on by Cathy herself. These fighting serpents helped Cathy more than all the words loving people said to her; she could *see* the battle she was engaged in, and she could use the energy from the dream where she knew "the battle had not been lost."

We can amplify the dream with general amplification also, since it is presented in the powerful, mysterious battle of snakes. In *Symbols of Transformation in Dreams* we have written about the snake as a symbol which, while including the sexual meaning which Freud taught us, is not limited to that significance. Snakes in dreams present the challenge to integrate our instinctual base with some new level of consciousness. Snakes represent power and they represent danger. Their chthonic nature, close to the earth and cold-blooded, is partly responsible for their numinous fascination. They have long been associated with healing. You might say that Cathy's dream has given her a different scene like Eden, where the depressive snake which would pull her down into the hell of despair is being battled and beaten by the brave little chthonic feminine self.

Three years or so later, Cathy had become aware that the two fighting snakes were even more inherent in her patterns of functioning than the comfort which came to her in sorrow. Though her black depression had been strongest after her tragic loss, it was always there, waiting to fight off her true self, represented by the courageous little Mary-snake. The fighting snakes were a lifelong core image for Cathy.

The Wounded Pastoral Counselor

Another core image came to a pastoral counselor from a dream he had a few days after he made a major decision which had been extremely difficult. He decided that, for the integrity of his life journey, he had to leave the church with which he was affiliated. He had been deeply wounded by church leaders for years, and it was simply time to call a halt to it. He wrote letters to his denomination renouncing his connection with them. He did not know where he would go, nor what the effect on his life and his career would be, but he felt an inner necessity to take this action. A few nights later, he dreamed:

> I was in a cathedral, desiring communion. It felt good to be there with the other people. The celebrant was S., a broken

priest, who celebrated with joy. I took communion and was at peace. After the service, S. showed me the floor at the rear of the church. He said that though the flooring stone looked worn and sunken, it was a strong church according to engineering inspections recently held. He brushed away the top slabs to show granite pillars which went to the center of the earth. I was surprised and awe-struck. I looked at the facade of the church and realized that it was a medieval structure which might fall off. I also realized that if it fell off it would not affect the sanctuary, since it was upon a foundation connecting it to the center of the earth.

Even before we know his associations with the images in the dream, we can feel the impact of several parts of it. Knowing what he has just been through, I am particularly struck by the poignant phrase "desire communion." It seems to me to refer not only to his wanting to receive the Lord's supper, but also the deep communion and community with God and the company of believers which he longs for and fears he may have lost. The other powerful phrase, of course, is that right at the end—that nothing would "affect the sanctuary, since it was upon a foundation connecting it to the center of the earth." We can share his awe just from the images themselves.

The dreamer felt the peace of the dream on waking. Even though he had just severed his connection with his own church, he understood the dream to say that his faith was his core and was deeply anchored in Christianity, which is deeply anchored in history and reality. He said, "It is the center of my being."

S., whom the dream described as "a broken priest" was in fact an ex-Roman Catholic priest (not the dreamer's church) who had left the priesthood some years before to marry and have a family. He was seriously ill—hence his "brokenness" in the dream. The dreamer also realized from the dream that he could allow wounded religious leaders to minister to him. The dream helped him no longer expect a perfection from them, nor from himself. So he himself could also minister, though he had experienced his own brokenness. In the language of the dream, he himself could be a broken priest and still celebrate with joy.

He also learned from the dream symbolism that to change the appearance—the facade—of the church is not to lose its depth, continuity, and power. One can let go of the past and still have something from it bigger than what was relinquished. He could, in the core image of the dream, make a new kind of connection with his faith—the center of his own being.

The Wedding Garment

The next example of a core image from a dream came to me in an odd way. It was also unusual in that the dream had been a source of pain to the dreamer for over twenty years—in large part, I think, because of some of the mistaken interpretations that popular folklore about dreams suggests.

I had preached a sermon one Sunday on a parable in Matthew's Gospel, chapter 22, usually referred to as the parable of the wedding garment. In the parable Jesus described the kingdom of heaven as being like a king who gave a marriage feast for his son, but none of the invited guests would come. Even after a repeated invitation, none of the guests would come, making light of the feast and giving varied excuses.

I had spoken in my sermon of imagining the wedding feast for the king's son: the feast with the fat calves, the festive air, the plenty—pressed down and running over—the music and dancing, the fine wine and food, the beautiful clothes, the laughter and merry making.

In connection with the refusal of people to go to this grand party, I was reminded of a great line from the old novel and movie *Auntie Mame* (cleaned up a little). Auntie Mame tells her nephew: "Patrick, life is a banquet and most people are starving to death." So the wedding feast seemed to me to be a physical image of a spiritual longing, the kind of joy, deep joy, that the scripture talks about: wonderful plans of God from time immemorial, death swallowed up forever, tears wiped away, the peace that passes understanding— the God of our deepest hopes.

Yet Jesus' parable continues with the king's servants being treated shamefully and even killed by those who didn't want to come to this feast. The king reacted with anger and revenge and then sent his servants to invite everyone they saw in the streets, both good and bad, to come to the banquet, so the wedding hall was filled with guests.

The parable suggested to me that the wedding feast (the kingdom of heaven) is open to us all, but what we all do is make trivial excuses not to come. The Medical Mission Sisters have a song about this parable, and the chorus goes: "I cannot come to the banquet, don't trouble me now. I have married a wife. I have bought me a cow. I have fields and commitments that cost a pretty sum. Pray hold me excused, I cannot come."[4]

I had also confessed in the sermon that my heart sank when I saw the Gospel passage that I would have to preach on that Sunday because of the next part of the parable. The king comes into the hall where the guests are gathered and sees one man without a wedding garment. He orders his servants to bind the man and cast him into outer darkness where "men will weep and gnash their teeth."

I had never really worked through that passage to a meaning which felt consistent to me with my understanding of our relationship to God. So in my sermon preparation I had been pushed to some troubled probing—what in the world was that wedding garment about? For me it had been one of those puzzling passages that I had put on the shelf to worry about later. What could it mean that you have to be dressed right to come to the messianic banquet?

I had suggested my best answer—still none too profound—that we bring ourselves in honesty (the good and the bad in ourselves) and we have to be willing in that honesty to celebrate with God. We have to be willing to let God see us just as we are, without excuses; we have to be willing to let God show us ourselves clearly.

At any rate, at the coffee hour after the service a gentle, soft-spoken, gray-haired woman spoke to me hesitantly about a worry she had, encouraged to do so by my struggle with the wedding garment parable. She told me that twenty years before she had dreamed that she saw lying on the ground a white jacket, and in the dream she just looked at it and left it on the ground.

She said that as soon as she woke, she thought, "The wedding garment." She was an active churchgoer who knew her Bible, and the thought which struck her immediately was: "Why did I leave it there? Why didn't I put it on?" Steeped, as so many of us are, in the reifying-absolutist interpretation of dreams, she felt immediately that the dream meant she was a person who rejected coming to God's feast, despite her conscious intention. The garment lay right there in the dream, but she never picked it up and put it on. She said she wept bitterly at this realization. She never told the dream to anyone, but she never forgot it either.

She told me about the dream because my sermon had opened a sort of hope in her that somehow she might be rid of that twenty-year anxiety. I told her that dreams did not present us with a finalized fate from which we could not escape. I trusted her association with the wedding garment as being the white robe or jacket in her dream, but still did not think that meant she was fated to live out her dream image.

I told her that dreams presented us with some part of ourselves that we were unconscious of or not living out, but we still had the possibility of choices. I said, in the imagery of her dream, that she could pick up the garment and put it on now. She was a reserved person, shy and quiet, so she said very little then, except to thank me for the idea that she had a choice.

Her husband, a more outspoken person, was amazed. He said, "But you never told me!" He also was surprised that when she had received "the baptism of the Holy Spirit" the worry had remained with her—urging her to affirm that this experience of the presence of God with her had healed everything. She quietly said that the worry had never left her, despite all the events of the twenty years.

She wrote me a note the next week in which she said, "The time you spent with me was enough to lift my spirit to walk freely with my Lord. I know He wants us to be free, and walk with our head up high, but my head was hanging low and my heart was too, because I felt guilty. Why was my little white robe on the ground? So I picked it up and thanked Him and put it on. And I thank you because you helped me put it on and I love wearing it—it makes me feel good—*good* in the robe. What a joy! Please know what you have done for me—it was no small thing!"

Of all the experiences I have had of talking to people about their dreams, this was for me one of the most astonishing—both in seeing the worry this dear woman had carried for all those years and also in seeing how simply telling her that the dream presented her with a choice to make could have such an effect on her peace of mind.

It is seldom possible to understand the depth and power that other persons' core images have for their lives, but this woman's gracious note catches the release of energy in her. She knew at the feeling level the importance of the wedding garment image for herself, and she wept because she thought she had failed in her faith. The level of energy she felt released was comparable to the level of sorrow she had carried. She was delighted for me to share her story, though shyly surprised that her experience might be interesting to anyone else.

In these examples, the dreamers knew the importance of the images in their dreams. They carried great intensity to the dreamers on waking. The woman wept for her wedding garment and carried this sorrow for twenty years. Cathy's image of the snakes fighting released her from her black depression for the first time since her fiancé's death. The wounded pastoral counselor spent years and energy agonizing over his relationship to the church, and a deep peace came to him through his dream presenting him with the comfort of his inner cathedral and its deep foundations. Monnica let her son move back home and kept up her hope for nine years until his baptism.

Like other core images, those which appear in dreams may last a lifetime or they may be prominent for only a certain period. Whichever they are, the images have that continuing quality of picking up something from the past, connecting it with the present, and pointing the potential for the future.

The images themselves can act as transformers. People may get the *energy* to carry through with a change in themselves from a compensatory dream in which they appeared to be like the change or in which they acted out the transformation they want. Even if the dream is not interpreted or understood or even thought about, still the energy may be released in them.

Material from dreams is organic to the dreamer and it is objective. They know they dreamed it, and they know they can't make it come up in dreams. That intersection is where the power is, or put in religious language, that's where God is in the situation.

They're the only one in the world who can know they dreamed it. It is really theirs. It comes out of them. The only source of it is their report. There is real ownership of it, and that is powerful.

Once you start getting the understanding that if you dream something, it is part of you or else you couldn't dream it, then you begin to get allies, including the challengers. The power the dreamer cannot feel will show up in the dreams.

The Self is the dream-maker, Jung says. Christians and some other theists may say that dreams are God's forgotten language. Whichever language you use, you are saying there is a power in the universe that cares about me. As you start doing dream work, you experience that caring center. This is why some people can get a sense of their own meaning from dream work. They begin to get a sense that they matter.

So it's both experiencing your own inner strength and the objectivity of that—I'm not just making this up; this really has an objective validity to it—*and* you're experiencing, as the process theologians might say, being lured forward into your future, being lured forward into the potential for you, into your own revelation. The Mary-snake, undifferentiated as it is, had the power to lure Cathy toward her future.

In addition, as will be seen from several of the examples in previous chapters, dreams can be a prime way of carrying forward core images originally recognized in other ways. Steve, who realized he was the sacrificial goat for his family, began his realization with the group work on a dream. As will appear in chapter 9, he also continued to develop his understanding of how this played out in his life from dreams. Linda Leonard used dreams as a part of her work with her images of fire and creativity, as did Laura, whose dream of the cleansing fire helped her overcome her taped-mouth fears. Ken's childhood dream of the train going in circles connected with his pain over his family role as sacrificial victim. Diane's dreams were clarifying indicators in her journey to transform her core image of the bloody crucifixion so that she could be free of her overscrupulous guilt.

In fact, though I have divided the search for core images into chapters and focused thus on only a few of the major places to watch for their emergence, this is a false division for purposes of illustration only. There is really no division.

The identification of core images and continued work with them will always involve seeing the significance of the images in all parts of our lives and their showing up in many different guises. Images which are central to our personality will pervade our material the way a theme of music pervades a symphony, and they will be played on all the instruments of our human orchestra.

· PART II ·

Core Images and Psychotherapy

·6·

Operational Theory

As a pastoral counselor, I tend to understand psychotherapy—the healing of the soul—in terms both of psychology and theology. I thus find it difficult to separate the
operational background of core image work into its psychological
components on the one hand and its theological components on
the other. There are areas which are discrete, of course, but more
areas in which they overlap. Thus when I talk about the operational
theory of core image work, I speak about both theology and psychology.

In fact, though I could not have identified this truth at the time,
my own adult conversion to Christianity had started me on the
road to symbolic work ten years before I encountered Jungian
theory. This symbolic focus in my theology is partly, of course,
because I began my theological perspective from the sacramental,
Anglican view which understands theology as coming from three
essential sources, the Anglican "three-legged stool": scripture, tradition, and reason. When those three come together, then Anglicans
can make a theological statement, and they will try to come up
with a sacramental observance or liturgy to practice it. I think the
testing of such statements also includes the John Wesley/Methodist
focus on human experience, which many twentieth-century theologians stress (William Temple, Paul Tillich, John Knox, Karl Rahner,
John Macquarrie, to name a few). Obviously, when human experience is a theological factor, we are also in the area of psychology.

In discussing the personality theory that lies behind work with
core images, as I said at the beginning, I am not decrying other

theoretical approaches to personality and psychotherapy or using this symbolic approach in an exclusivist way. I have found some theories more helpful than others, as I am sure is the case for other people as well, but that does not, of course, mean they are necessarily thereby more helpful to some other counselor. There are some theories, as I will mention later, which I think tend to vitiate true symbolic work, and I will argue against them, but most observed human data can be approached symbolically.

In the material which follows I have no pretensions to making any complete or systematic statement of either theology or personality theory, but I am attempting to delineate the assumptions in both which lie behind core image work.

Individuality and Vocation

A primary precept behind symbolic work with core images is that, as James Ashbrook puts it, there is "a stubborn oddness at the heart of things." No one can ever know what another person's life is to be, no matter how wise you have become, or, put another way, "[T]he journey of each soul is unique and unrepeatable."[1] This is the religious presupposition about human personality which lies behind core image work from the symbolic perspective and is, in effect, part of the operational theology of living the symbolic life. Operational theology looks beyond an individual's stated theology to the mental pictures and images of God and of how the world works, and to the values we actually practice in our lives.

The second primary precept is that each of us has a vocation or calling, though the discernment of that vocation may be difficult. I am certainly not using "vocation" in the limited sense of our job or profession. Nor am I using it in the sometime common Christian, limited sense of applying only to ministers, priests, or nuns. There have been various times in the history of the church when to "have a vocation" meant precisely this limited view. Even in churches which support the "priesthood of all believers," the phrase "going into the church" frequently is used for entering professional ordained ministry rather than joining the church or being baptized.

I think vocation is for every person and involves lives lived in fullness, whether short or long, whether famous or unsung, remembered or forgotten. The miracle of human life which I have observed convinces me that we each matter to the world, whether the world ever knows it or not. We can make a difference, and living our most true lives begins when we begin to see what God sees in us. Paul Pruyser says what sets a vocation apart is that "a sense of purpose is attached to [one's] doings which validates [one's] existence under [the] Creator." This, he adds, enables vocation to be "melioristic—it is putting one's talents to work as a participant in the process that moves the universe toward increasing integrity."[2]

My focus on individuality accords with the theological understanding of each person as a child of God, as important as if an only child. Each person's vocation then is seen as an individual call from God, who calls us by name, with the call being exercised in various communities or contexts, some specifically religious, some secular. As Bonhoeffer said, we cannot predetermine how the image of Christ will appear to a person, but must allow the image of Christ to develop in that person as that person needs.

This is the belief inherent in a favorite story of mine, of the old rabbi who prayed, "Oh, God, make me like Abraham!" only to be answered, "But I already have an Abraham." This is the kind of respect for the individual soul and the individual journey which I think is profoundly religious.

The best of spiritual-direction material emphasizes this kind of individuality and vocation. As one writer on spiritual direction put it: "The director, then, must have a high regard and deep reverence for souls, and for the designs of God for each soul."[3] Another identifies the qualities required of a spiritual director as including first "the ability to reverence the infinite variety of human beings."[4] As another says, "To direct a soul is to direct a world which has more secrets and diversities, more perfections and rarities, than the material universe."[5]

Spiritual directors at best know that the source of direction does not lie with them, but with God, so they know their open listening stance is their most important contribution. In practice, of course, it has not always been so, and spiritual directors also sometimes fail to respect this radical individuality of each person's soul. I am not speaking of that which is always done well, but of theological assumptions.

Jung also taught a kind of very specific and individualized vocation to wholeness. His concept of the organizing center, which he called the Self, as the God-image within each of us is helpful in stressing the individualized specificity of each person's wholeness and vocation. "Self" used in this sense is something quite different from "self" as many other personality theorists use it. If "self" means myself or yourself, Jung would use the word *ego*, the conscious part of ourselves we usually call "I."

This "Self" of Jung's theory is outside consciousness, perhaps even "outside" our psyches—he viewed its "location" as unknown. What could be seen, he thought, was the result on our psyches of some guiding force, which, he once commented, has usually been called "God." Jung thus postulated an organizing center which produces our symbolic images and moves the individual more and more toward that individual's potential wholeness.

Jung named the path toward our wholeness, in an inspired word choice, by the term "individuation." By individuation he means something more than merely separating oneself away from people with whom one is enmeshed—a common use of the word today—though he would certainly include that meaning. He means that empirically we can observe that the symbols in our lives operate purposively.

The major task of symbolic work is to help people learn to reflect on what they do and why, thus enhancing their ability to be intentional, conscious, and effective in their lives, without losing touch with the charism of their original call to be. Healing and creativity require both personal reflection and the stimulation and evocation of sharing the ideas and experiences of others. Whether carried out alone, with trusted helpers, in families, or in other communities, symbolic work *is* religious work (in the larger sense of the word *religious*) because it looks for the meaning that images carry.

Getting in touch with our life's meaning is a basic religious task, and core image work assumes that our life's meaning will involve a vocational path to which we are called. To carry out our life's meaning, we need to be aware of the stories we tell about ourselves, as well as the contextual influences that affect who we are. We need to be more aware of the strategies we use to engage the world and how these help or hinder our life's meaning.

Depth psychology, using all the resources of both conscious and unconscious, looks for this sense of personal meaning or vocation. The initial goal in depth psychology work is to connect you to the unconscious, to make an intentional dialogue between conscious and unconscious. People who live on the surface of their lives without reflecting on why they do what they do are living only in the world of the conscious ego. From Freud's discovery of what we now call "Freudian slips" this world of the conscious ego has been put in perspective. When the unconscious impinges on consciousness, we find ourselves doing and saying things other than what we consciously intended, frequently to our embarrassment. When we listen to the messages from the unconscious and begin to dialogue with them and try to understand them, Jung and many other depth psychologists think these symbols will lead us beyond our feared negatives into our possible futures, to our individuation.

This is related to the theological position that God is luring each of us toward our true selves. This is not to say that God and the unconscious are the same, but to say that the immanence of God comes to us through the unconscious. Core image work, which trusts the images in each person's life to lead toward their wholeness, honors the transcendent component. It is desperately important that we as helpers do not usurp the role of the Self or the Holy Spirit, for, as one early spiritual director put it, *"[D]ivine grace . . .* conducts souls in spiritual dispositions by an almost infinite variety of paths and fashions" (emphasis added).[6]

The growth and healing and learning in symbolic core image work at best recognize this transcendent component in the work— something far beyond the mutual capabilities of both people. With these images we have the framework to identify and expect this divine help. We do not bear the burden of ultimacy. We can see ourselves as "planters" and "waterers" and wait expectantly for the providential mystery of growth.

This was one aspect of Jungian thought which attracted me early on, as it seemed to me consistent with the Christian concept of each individual soul as being of primary importance and having a personal and meaningful vocation. Christian spiritual development urges self-knowledge under the guidance of God; Jungian thought points to increasing consciousness as the way to wholeness. This view presupposes that "wholeness" or "working out our own salvation in fear and trembling" does not involve a particular formula of development, but the goal of the work is the full development of each individual in a particularized way.

Furthermore, Jungian thought teaches us that inner work involves not only retrospective work dealing with the past, but prospective work dealing with the present moving into the future. The Self pulls us into our futures, as in religious language we say that the Holy Spirit calls us. This invokes the aspect of the inner work which is not yet, but can come to be in our lives.

This is the enlargement of personality and life which is held out by religious life, by Jungian individuation, and by growth models in general. Though Jung was the first psychological theorist I encountered who worked with this kind of personalized growth model, there are, of course, many other theorists today with this same goal of personal meaning making. I mention two others.

A similar view of the individual is taught by Roberto Assagioli in his theories of psychosynthesis, among whose precepts is the recognition of the uniqueness of each individual, requiring what he calls "differential psychosynthesis," or a different combination of the many techniques of therapy into a new method for each person. Assagioli's many techniques of transformation have as a goal progressive as well as regressive work, beyond the removal of symptoms. One of his treatment methods arises from the use in therapy of what he calls "individual or spontaneous symbols."[7] His work with "sub-personsonalities" is a way of naming, and thus identifying, our ambivalence because of the various parts of ourselves which pull us in various directions. Though there may be types which are common to others, no one will have quite the same set as another.

As I understand object relations theory, it also has this possibility of seeing individuals more discretely than its psychoanalytic parent sometimes does. Against the general background of the theory of personality which focuses on the relation between self (ego) and other, the specifics of the particular objects to which the evolving person relates carry primary importance. Not only is this relational interaction necessary for people to become people, but this action of becoming is seen as involving the quest for meaning, even for transcendence, seen as a basic human need. This appears to me to offer the same possibility of honoring the individual life experience and its possibility of transformation.

Lastly, though I have stressed the individual nature of this symbolic work, I intend that focus only to emphasize that each person is different, never to pretend that any of us operates our lives in a vacuum. As indicated elsewhere in this work, our individuality is always lived in relationship and our healing is always lived into in the context of our various communities of experience. Our core images themselves come in part from these contexts and relationships, and the vocations to which they lead us will be carried out in the world of relationships and communities. By the focus on individuality I mean that the particular way they are constellated in each life will be different, even in the same families or communities.

We all have needs for freedom and independence and needs for affiliation and attachment. I see the rhythm between these needs operating in a circular or spiral movement. A healthy context (or a healing context which helps us recover from unhealthy ones) supports and encourages freedom and development, enabling independence. A truly independent person in turn is able to make healthy attachments and affiliations, without being caught in fused or enmeshed dependencies. You can enter this circle of healing in either place, and the rhythm goes on throughout life.   .

To recognize the individuality of each person and to see each person's vocation in life as distinctive is not to say that any of us lives our life alone; loneliness is in fact a primary problem of modern life. Until we can learn to live our transformations in the daily world in which we find ourselves, the work is incomplete. "The daily round, the common task"—these are where life and transformation are carried out.

Possibility of Redemption

Another theoretical underpinning of core image work is that human beings have a tendency, if nothing gets in the way, toward healing and wholeness. The body heals itself after injury; medical treatment helps to get the body to the place where nothing interferes with that healing—even to help healing along; but the surgeon who sets the bone does not heal the bone. The body heals itself, given the opportunity. Psychologically, the same process can be observed, if nothing gets in the way.

Nondirective play therapy stresses that even in young children, the ability is there for the solutions to problems to come from within the individual. The reason that play therapists can and must be permissive, in that theory, is "based upon a philosophy of human relationships which stresses the importance of the individual as a capable, dependable human being who can be entrusted with the responsibility for himself."[8] The child's play is understood to be symbolic of the child's feelings, and if the therapist does interpret the play to the child, the response is always to include the symbol the child used, because from the child's own symbols the solutions come.

Constructive developmental theory recognizes that "human beings are continually in motion with a yearning toward balance, equilibrium, and wholeness which is extraordinarily creative in character, seeking meaningful life. The capacity for growth and healing that it reveals, even when the cost is great, manifests the power of life itself." Such theorists as Robert Kegan and Sharon Parks identify this activity as belonging to the soul—beyond ego and beyond client and therapist—"a dynamic power, moving unseen, which seeks to creatively protect and recompose the self in relation to self, the social world, and the cosmos, so as to weave the person into fitting, meaningful re-connection with all of life."[9]

Family systems theory is based on the same kind of positive view, asserting that each individual has an energy which moves the individual forward in progressive stages of growth unless the energy is restricted. The family is also seen as a living organism, and families also have an energy to move forward in progressive stages if their members are free to interact in ways that do not block the flow of creative energy.[10]

The same focus on a purposive tendency toward healing in the psyche has been explored by theorists from several schools with regard to schizophrenic and psychotic patients. R. D. Laing claimed that not only the instincts were repressed by our civilization, but also "any form of transcendence." He equates being "on the side of transcendence" with being on the side of "genuine freedom, and of true human growth." From all this he urged a psychotherapy which listened to and respected even the most delusional material as relevant to healing.[11]

A fascinating study of the lengthy case of the patient Mary Barnes using Laing's theories was jointly written by patient and psychiatrist. The house in which this treatment was done was set up to see "whether psychosis was our culture's means of archetypal renewal of the inner self," which, Laing felt, many other cultures provided evidence for. A whole community worked for several years on her wholeness, raising for me when I read it the religious conviction that all their effort was worth it and that, if we only cared enough, anyone could be "saved" from disintegration. The therapist's conviction, with which he began work with Mary, was that "Every patient is entitled to a fresh and unbiased study of his or her experiential world." Mary herself calls this therapy place "the sort of place I want, something sacred, full of *love*."[12]

John Weir Perry, following Jungian personality theory, uses research and case material to assert that there is an archetypal basis in brief reactive psychosis, which is itself a renewal process that can facilitate a rebirth process of healing. His teaching served as the basis for establishment of several alternative residential facilities for the treatment of young adults undergoing brief reactive psychoses. Incidentally, Perry points out that in the modern handling of the individuation process by many analysts, the social concerns of kinship with one's fellow beings are the most likely to be neglected.[13]

My focus is obviously on the intrapsychic paradigm, and my work has primarily been with individuals, but these treatment modalities are community based and operate with many of the insights of systems thought. Even in work with individuals I have been aided by the insights of family systems, and I have a notion that the symbolic approach is also useful in a corresponding way in family therapy, which works with a similar redemptive possibility. As family clinicians discover core family images, they bear the same potential for transformation toward the family change which family therapists seek to activate.

The theological corollary of both individual and family work is the belief that God is on the side of healing and wholeness. The God who calls us into our futures is a God in favor of redemption, of our being set free. This is an incarnational faith, but I think it is not limited to Christianity with its incarnated redeemer.

The God of the Hebrew scriptures enters history; the religions of the Book encounter a living God who calls them to behaviors that are redemptive for the individual, the community, and the world. Jeremiah hears the word of the Lord calling him to be a prophet to the nations, "Before I formed you in the womb I knew you, and before you were born I consecrated you" (Jeremiah 1:5). Isaiah is called from the time of his initial vision on throughout his life; the biblical world is a world of people in contact with God who continually calls them to personal and communal action, even when they resist, like Jonah.

The thrust of Buddhism, though not theistic in the same way, is, I believe, a work toward enlightenment taking place in the plan of things by a kind of cosmic extension of the deepest moral law, so that true happiness, for example, consists in connecting with something that transcends purely instinctual urges. The major world religions are all, I think it can be safely said, in favor of redemption, or, as William James urges, there is a "certain uniform deliverance in which all religions appear to meet." He describes this deliverance thus: "The solution is a sense that *we are saved from the wrongness* [in ourselves] by making proper connection with the higher powers."[14]

Some see this movement as a drive to life, growth, health, or self-actualization. Some see a transcendent component, either from God, the Self (in the God-image sense), or by the providential grace of the Holy Spirit through the redemptive action of Jesus Christ building on nature. Some see the movement as a combination of several or all of these.

I agree with Walter Conn that the concept of self-trancendence can enable pastoral counseling to integrate psychology and theology "by seeing them as two complementary interpretations of the single radical drive of the human spirit." As he points out, "A psychology that understands self-realization as self-transcendence and a theology that recognizes the gospel as a call to self-transcendence require no connecting bridge of reconciliation, only the discovery of their intrinsic unity as interpretations of the same fundamental human drive for self-transcendence."[15]

Whatever belief system you accept, however, the movement is purposive and redemptive; it operates with the virtue of hope. In any of these systems, core images can be seen as containing purposive and redemptive potential. So, it might be said that another tenet of the theology underlying symbolic work is that redemption is possible and that some measure of individual choice is involved in claiming that redemptive possibility. There is meaning in our lives and we have some choice of whether and to what extent we incarnate our meaning.

Jung uses a helpful image for the kind of individually designed growth he urged, this focus on coming to consciousness, on increased awareness of the motives which lie behind one's behavior. His image is that of islands rising up out of the sea, growing larger, and finally merging with one another into peninsulas and continents. It is as if in the work we do as we make the spiritual journey or walk with people and work with them on their increasing reality, we are helping them make land out of the dark sea. We have joined them in the great work of continuing creation.

Original Sin and Original Blessing in Psychological Theory: Freud and Rogers

Of course, not all psychological or theological theorists accept such an individualized and hopeful approach. Terry Cooper compares different schools which have been influential in pastoral counseling, identifies differing understandings of human personality, and gives insight as to some of the reasons reconciliation is difficult.[16]

He argues persuasively that Carl Rogers's battle against the established medical community as the sole controller of the helping professions is akin to Martin Luther's battle against the established religious community as the sole controller of religious dogma. He paints a compelling picture of the two men fighting lonely battles on behalf of the belief that human beings can be trusted both to read scripture (Luther) and to move in the direction of mental health (Rogers).

Cooper places Rogers in a diametrically oppositional position to Freud, based on their basic beliefs in the nature of human beings. Rogers believed that the basic tendency of human beings, "when given an atmosphere of acceptance and freedom, can be trusted." Therapy then consists of inviting people to become their *real* selves, as opposed to the incongruent self, where people are strangers to themselves. Rogers believed that the congruent person "is self-trusting, self-directing, and positively oriented."

Freud, on the other hand, believed human beings to be, "at their core, . . . destructive, self-centered, uncivilized, and driven by the energies of sex and aggression." Only by sublimation of these drives into socially acceptable activities could anything good come out of human beings. Freud found little good in human beings, being quoted, in one of his "seasoned" statements as believing of people that "most of them are trash, no matter whether they publicly subscribed to this or that ethical doctrine or none at all."

Cooper sees this fundamental disagreement as the basis of the tensions in the field of pastoral counseling. He says no two thinkers have affected pastoral counseling more than Rogers and Freud, yet their basic assumptions (and the therapy arising from them) are in complete opposition. He describes an all-too-familiar scene of a supervisor from one school being concerned about a supervisee operating out of the other theory. Cooper argues that no "comfortable attitude of eclecticism" can reconcile the self-contradictory position of these two assumptions.

Yet Cooper closes on this interesting note:

> This opposition between the Freudian pessimism about human depravity and the Rogerian optimism about human possibility represents the creative tension that is so basic to pastoral counseling. Both men were astute observers of human behavior. One can theologize on the basis of either perspective. Yet it is as impossible to reconcile their views as it was to reconcile the perspective of Luther and the counterreformers.[17]

Then, after posing the questions raised by the opposing views with reference to the practice of therapy, Cooper concludes his article thus: "These are the ongoing, difficult questions with which pastoral counseling must wrestle. And it has been Carl Rogers, more than any other figure, who has reflected Luther's bold invitation to reexamine these old questions."

I assume this means that he comes down on the side of Rogers, and I must say it has always been difficult for me to reconcile Freud's theological statements with the practice of pastoral counseling. In fact, Cooper clarifies the theology which leans comfortably toward Freudian practice by identifying Freud's view of the total depravity of humankind, so perhaps Freud is also relevant to some Reformation thought.

I was reminded as I read Cooper of a lecture that an American Jungian analyst, Clare Thompson, gave at the Jung Institute in Zurich in the mid-1960s. She placed Jungian practitioners in a quadrated square with those who followed Freud, Rogers, and Skinner filling the other squares of the quadrant. In one direction the quadrant was formed by separating the theorists who believed in and worked with the unconscious, Freud and Jung, from those who did not, Skinner and Rogers.

In the other direction, she placed those who believed that the personhood of the therapist was a part of the therapeutic process and thus were themselves "in" the process, as opposed to those who believed that the therapist as a person was to remain "outside" the process. In the former, of course, she placed Rogers and Jung; in the latter, Freud and Skinner. Her point was that Jungian work had something in common with Freud and something in common with Rogers, but very little with Skinner.

As I read Cooper's arguments, then, I had before me the memory of a quadrant which, if not precisely reconciling between Freud and Rogers, at least pointed to the fact that Jungian theory and practice had something in common with both. These theorists are not, I would argue, as hopelessly irreconcilable as Cooper presented Rogers and Freud to be, though the division he points to has certainly been so experienced in much of pastoral counseling.

What then can bring them together, if Cooper presents the personality theories of the two men fairly, as I think he does? I think the reconciling factor is seen in the subsequent developments of other theorists, who saw human personality in increasingly complicated terms. Cooper is right in noting that both Freud and Rogers were astute observers of human personality. As scholars and clinicians have turned their attention to the study of humanity, the complexity is discovered to be manifold. It is that very complexity which enables us to say that each theorist sees some aspects of the truth. We need not deny the accuracy in the observations of any of them in order to endorse the accuracy of others. Many of the theorists who come initially out of the Freudian school illustrate this by having moved far beyond Freud in defining the complexity of human personality—Heinz Kohut, the object relations theorists, and Robert Assagioli, to mention but a few.

Jung broke with Freud precisely over this point. He felt that Freud had correctly identified unconscious processes in human functioning, but that his own drive theory was too limited. People were more complicated than Freud's theory provided for. Many subsequent neo-Freudians have also illuminated additional complexities which Freud did not allow for, as mentioned.

In Jung's case, the break came from Jung's belief that the unconscious consisted not only of forgotten, suppressed, or repressed material from the personal life history, but also contained material which had never been part of the person's life. He thus postulated two "layers" of the unconscious, calling the first the "personal unconscious" and the deeper, nonpersonal layer the "collective unconscious" or "objective psyche." It was this latter theory which caused Freud to plead with Jung not to abandon the "sexual dogma," but to defend it against the tide of occultism which Freud feared would engulf civilization.[18]

Jung also feared for civilization, but he proposed a different way of dealing with the threats. His answer was increasing consciousness, but a consciousness based upon his observation that human unconsciousness not only contained significant images from the past for understanding the present. He argued that material from the deeper layers of the unconscious also had significance for the person's future. Borrowing the language of process theologians, we could say fairly that Jung felt the unconscious center was "luring" each of us toward our future as well.

In other words, using Cooper's comparison of Freud and Rogers, we might say that Jung accepted the "original sin" with which Freudian theory is so consonant; but he also found in human personality that "original blessing" which made Rogers trust human possibility. His therapy uses the material from the unconscious, no matter how depraved, but also finds from the unconscious the thrust toward human potential for creativity.

He felt that we live in this tension, each of us, and that consciousness enables us to make more creative choices in our lives toward our *real* self. He thought, along with Rogers, the subsequent human potential movement, the growth model of human development, and such family theorists as Virginia Satir, especially, that pathology is linked to the inability to reach our potential. These theorists all teach that human beings are geared toward fulfillment, that there is a thrust toward wholeness in each of us; but Jung, at least, never forgot his roots in the Freudian vision of the possibility of depravity in ourselves. Never forget, he urged, that you are dangerous.

·7·

Diagnosis

When I first approached diagnosis in terms of core images, I confess I did so partly with tongue in cheek. The term itself seemed to me almost antithetical to the focus on specificity inherent in core image work, where it is more accurate to speak of a symbolic approach than of a diagnosis. Furthermore, as Paul Pruyser pointed out in urging new forms of pastoral diagnosis, "diagnosis" has been all but absorbed by medicine. He is at pains to point out that diagnosis is actually a much more general term, meaning discernment and discrimination used to distinguish one condition from another in any field of knowledge.[1] Therefore, despite my initial tongue-in-cheek attitude, it seems appropriate to follow Pruyser's lead and reclaim diagnosis.

Diagnosis, as commonly used, almost always involves some systemic, general structure of understanding human health and sickness. Insofar as it is generalized, it cannot be specific to the person. It is the old problem of the one and the many. If we assert that there are generalized structures which can be defined, are we denying individuality? My answer might be put in these terms: yes, we are denying individuality, but we must.

Human complexity is too vast for us to deal with unless we have some categories of understanding. We are also a part of humankind and of nature in general. The events of our lives can be generalized; there are only so many experiences that people can have, and so patterns of experience and response can be identified. We belong to one another, and we will always try to put human experience into structures, but we must never think that the structures contain the life itself. I do think our diagnostic structures are more helpful when they contain a low level of abstraction and thus stay closer to the individual. One caution, then, for the diagnostician is not to misuse diagnostic categories in such a way as to deny individuality. This is the age-old danger of the Procrustean bed, where it becomes more important to make the "box" fit than to listen carefully to the person's life and story.

Dangers in Diagnosis

Perhaps the most bothersome danger in diagnosis is the danger of becoming authoritarian, of looking down one's nose, *de haut en bas*, of the all-knowing doctor or priest pronouncing what is best for the sick or sinful person. This is very tricky, because it does contain a partial truth—the doctor or priest is a trained expert in the categories of illness and sin. Yet too often in the past this has led to God-like projections upon the expert, who is supposed to "fix" the patient or penitent. It can leave out the fact that the person being "fixed" is the real expert; that person is living the life.

Tragedies like the Jonestown suicides have raised our consciousness about the dangers of too much power being placed in the hands of another human being in religious communities, though of course this consciousness is far from universal. The movement toward patient responsibility for one's own health has made some major changes in medical practice in recent years, and these changes work toward a mutuality which avoids authoritarianism. Though urged to do so by many writers and patient advocates, it is unclear how many times religious and medical authorities have sufficiently shed their paternalistic heritage to allow diagnosis and treatment to be a truly participatory enterprise which includes the patient or parishioner.

In conflicting fields of diagnosis with everyone claiming authority, it is all too often as if one person shouts, "This person is really sick," while another shouts, "This person can get well." Both are true, and the process I want to praise is one which is mutual, with two people or a team working together, each of whom knows some things which may prove helpful to the one who is client. A balance is needed.

Years ago I heard "teaching" defined as "being present when

learning takes place." I have found a helpful definition of therapy to be "being present when healing takes place." This is not to say that the therapist does nothing, but that all of who the therapist is enters the process, as well as the grace beyond both people. "Being truly present" involves all of them.

My own discomfort with diagnosis from the beginning of my counseling practice involves yet another danger, mentioned above—that somehow the person gets lost in the diagnosis. Joseph Wheelwright of San Francisco, psychiatrist and dean of American Jungian analysts, precisely catches my amorphous discomfort in this comment:

> In the same vein, I would like to comment that I think diagnosis is a terribly dangerous thing. I'm enormously opposed to it in the field of therapy because if I start diagnosing people, all the things I've read about anxiety states, or hysterical conversions, or schizophrenia, or manic-depressives, or whatever it might be, immediately come flooding into my head. It's as if I'd pushed a button, and all this knowledge pours through the floodgates and gets between me and the person I'm working with. I used to say that before I'd start work with a patient, I'd rush in and grab an eraser off the blackboard and scrub my cortex absolutely clean, so there would be nothing preconceived between me and the patient.[2]

There is also another danger for the clinician in diagnosing, implied in Joe Wheelwright's comment. That lies in the possible interference with the virtue of hope which an undue focus on pathology may engender, not only in the client, but also in the therapist. Jung identified this danger in a telling statement:

> To make a correct diagnosis, and to nod your head gravely at a bad prognosis, is the less important aspect of the medical art. It can even cripple your enthusiasm, and in psychotherapy enthusiasm is the secret of success.[3]

Lastly, but certainly significant, especially in psychiatric classification, is the risk that diagnostic labeling carries with it a stigmatizing effect. This is both a danger of society's view of the person and of the person's self-stigmatizing.[4] This in itself can seriously interfere with recovery. Any diagnostic interpretation which has this stigmatizing effect can become a source of blame and shame for the person being treated, adding to the weight of the burden. If the diagnosis is necessary for treatment and recovery, then, of course, this need takes precedence, but if treatment and recovery can be achieved with less stigma, that would be a distinct advantage to both therapist and the person being treated.

Nature of a Better Diagnosis

So much for some general negatives of diagnosis. To avoid them we would look for something which respects the mutuality of process between therapist and client, which does not get between counselor and client, which does not cripple enthusiasm for healing, which does not stigmatize the client, and which is more specific to the client.

Paul Pruyser lists a useful set of qualities which any system of diagnostic criteria should have, which I have condensed as follows: (1) readily recognizable; (2) able to produce empirical differentiations; (3) amenable to interview situations; (4) spanning conscious and unconscious levels, where possible; (5) containing phenomenological aptness, richness, and diversity to capture personal idiosyncrasies; and (6) able to yield a picture of the person, even if only a sketch or telling fragment, from which strategies for intervention can be developed.[5]

One way to make a more precise diagnosis which fits these criteria and avoids the negatives discussed above is to look for the specific core images which present themselves in the client's material, whether in the presenting issue or symptom, the observed patterns of dysfunction, the life history, the dreams, the emotional responses, or the stories idly told in the midst of sessions. The director or therapist may hear several possibilities which are then tested out as the work continues, but the diagnostic skill is in the sensitive listening, in a kind of symbolic alertness, and then in staying with the images as they unfold themselves. The core images have the role of carrying the life forward, and the helpers' theoretical process involves finding them and following them.

I think such a symbolic approach to identifying the areas which need healing can then be used against the background of many theories of personality and healing. Such theoretical structures will be in the background, and the specific core images will be in the foreground. The structures are part of the context in which the core image work is done, but the focus is kept specific through thinking of the core images themselves as the "diagnosis."

The core images as they are uncovered and revealed in each individual person's life are intrinsic, not extrinsic, internal, not external, to the person's life; they are an organic part of their personal life experience. Such symbols are completely exact for the person. They are tailor-made, not ready-made clothes. They fit perfectly. They are picture or event representations of who and how we are—not who and how anyone else is. They show us ourselves. They should be part of a respectable and responsible method of diagnosing, along with the more general systemic diagnoses.

A similar argument is urged by writers in feminist narrative theory. Feminist theory generally is based on the stories of women's lives, and the narratives of women's lives are the sources of the theory and research. This is the kind of specific attention to each person's life which core image work urges.

The feminist narrative theorists pay this attention to the construction of a given person's life, but they also recognize that each life is lived in many contexts. When the story of the individual's life is recounted, "The very act of giving form to a whole life . . . requires, at least implicitly, considering the meaning of the individual and social dynamics which seem to have been most significant shaping the life."[6] My own work through two decades of teaching Ira Progoff's intensive journal work has convinced me of the continuing value of such narrative work. It is as though people working with a journal begin to learn that they are living a story. Narratives open us to the continuity of our lives in new and healing ways.

This feminist view of the importance of always seeing the individual, but seeing that individual in context points to precisely the foreground-background emphasis which is needed in diagnosis. The goal of diagnosing according to core images is just this combination of individual and context, but core image work also stresses that life is to be seen symbolically as well as through whatever therapeutic lens the helper uses.

Let me now turn to some other theoretical constructs which can work well as partners and guides for therapists and directors in assessments using the symbolic approach of core images.

The Theory of Complexes

Jung's theory of complexes provides one helpful background, both for diagnosis and for treatment planning, considered in the next chapter. For the general public it is probably the most familiar and widely accepted of all his theories. I will deal with it at some length, both because it has proved so helpful to me and because it has so many similarities to possible core image work.

A complex is usually described as an emotionally toned cluster of elements in the psyche, consisting of a core of meaning surrounded by various images, opinions, and associations which gather around it, rather like an attracting magnet. It is usually noted as a complex when it gets out of your conscious control. Autonomous complexes—those carried to the nth degree—can operate separately from the intentional consciousness of a person in a way which is very much like biblical possession by evil spirits.

The ego itself, the center of consciousness, is a complex. No one is sure what causes the various aspects of personality to form themselves, but they seem to begin with a core. Some theorists think there is always a trauma or a particular traumatic incident at the center. Others think a single trauma is not sufficient, but must be reinforced by repetition. Systems theory has taught us, though, that repetition is probable in families and other institutions. A single remembered incident, such as those in the memories and family chapters (2 and 3, respectively), can be the key to the center of the complex, even though one's general life situation in the family and in the larger world is the more accurate center.

However the process begins, it seems to involve children making sense of life as best they can with whatever equipment they have available. Theorists have studied the age at which children begin to differentiate themselves from others in their world, and they have identified the stages at which they tend to adapt themselves to the various conflicts with which they must deal.

Complex theory suggests that they will build up a defense or an adaptation around the center. Then another situation will arise in which that defense is insufficient and another layer will build up and another and another, until the complex might be fairly depicted as a spiral with a connection all the way in to the middle. A complex thus has a powerful inner coherence and what Jung has called "its own wholeness."[7]

A complex reveals itself to us in a distortion of emotion. So when the area (or subject matter) of the complex is approached, strong emotions come. It is as if the center of meaning of the complex is circled around with all the defenses we have built up around the complex area, and they are connected as if by a wire. Then when something gets close to the outside of the spiral, even in an experience we don't immediately connect with the original subject matter, it creates an emotion in us, which quivers through our bodies in a physiological response or abreaction.

One way to think of a complex is as a flawed pattern of response to life in which one's emotions are controlled by the complex instead of being a spontaneous, uncluttered response to the situation. Thus, when the complex is constellated, one's emotions cannot be trusted to give true information, but must be tested against reality by some other means.

The images or dramas at the center of our complexes can also be seen as core images. The advantage of thinking in such a term as "core image," again, is that it stresses the individual nature of the complex. I find it more helpful to think in the specific terms of identifying core images which arise out of each life situation, precisely because they are so specific to the person.

For example, as I said in the case of Laura, the woman who taped up her mouth as a child, you could say that she had an inferiority complex or a mother complex, and both would be accurate. Yet the core image of taping up her mouth is more specific to Laura's wounding, to her pattern of present life, and to her overcoming the wounding by taking off the tape.

Developmental Theories

Developmental theories are another set of helpful patterns. Though I said earlier that wholeness does not involve a particular formula of development, there are of course many patterns we can discern which are common to human life, and extensive research has been done, beginning with Piaget, to test the stages of human development. I am helped by Erikson's stages of development and Carol Gilligan's feminist correctives of research data, as well as by Kohlberg's theories of moral development and the faith development theories of Jim Fowler, Sharon Parks, and others.

Of all these theorists, Robert Kegan's theories of the development of meaning-making in evolving ourselves may be the most useful with core images, overcoming various objections made to some other developmental theorists. His theory also avoids the Scylla and Charybdis of ego psychology and systems theory. Each of Kegan's stages of development involves both the person and the context (family, school, work, church) in which the person is embedded. He identifies the process of moving from one stage to another as the process of making meaning or growing.[8]

Joann Wolski Conn uses Kegan's theory in a fascinating illustrative diagnostic comparison with Paul Pruyser's pastoral diagnostic theory. She uses two of the same cases which Pruyser presented and imagines a pastoral counselor using Kegan's theories to work with the same people. Her work is incisive and very helpful in learning how to use Kegan in actual practice.[9]

Elizabeth Liebert supports the general usefulness of structural development theories, while recognizing objections to their "universal" claims. She stresses that this issue of the one and the many has been debated in philosophy for about twenty-five centuries, and she puts the problem this way: "Is there a basic unity underlying the diversity of things, or is each thing different from every other, with everything in constant flux?" She argues persuasively that combining feminist narrative theory and structuralist developmental theory is a "potentially fruitful avenue for attending to concrete persons in their particular contexts." She and the personal narrative group recognize the mythic aspect and even the way people "get things wrong" when telling their stories, but nonetheless claim that the truth of experience is worth careful attention and is revelatory of truths.[10]

As I said, I find Elizabeth Liebert's suggestions very cogent for core image work, particularly, as she says, for the clinician. The personal narrative group and others who work with narrative and story are also helpful insofar as they stress the individual connection with the story. Structural theories and other abstractions remain in the background.

Other Helpful Theories

One of the most important and useful set of theories is the generalized understanding given us by family systems in its varied models—psychodynamic, interpersonal, and intergenerational. This gives us a helpful view of the social and family context for therapeutic work, including work with individuals. I would have a hard time trying to distinguish identifying core images which are found in family patterns and memories from the family systems diagnostic method of seeing introjects as the internalized personal history of the family.

The specific symptom of the "identified patient," the family member who is "causing the trouble," can also be the symbol which holds the meaning of the family interaction. This is why family therapists prefer to work with the whole family rather than the troubling individual in order to try to change the family patterns. When their focus keeps generalized theory in the background and the specific content of the symptom in the foreground, they are also making a symbolic diagnosis such as I am trying to describe.

Some groups use image work to identify the symbol or spirit which motivates or dominates the group. For example, many churches today in preparation for calling a new minister will do a parish profile of what matters to the parish. People who work with corporations tell me they raise the question, "Where is the spirit of the corporation?" in workshops designed to help the corporation understand their mode of operations and goals—and to help them make appropriate changes. Many of us wish the governments of the world were more conscious of their core images and sensitive to the possible limitations and distortions inherent in them. The use of images is a way of understanding and relating to essential meaning and process.

Some of the theories which have grown out of psychoanalytic beginnings are helpful in diagnosing core images, at least as a part of the process. Object relations theory generally deals with the early internalization of relationships between oneself and the "other," particularly the mother. It sees the ego as the center of the personality, reaching out to other "objects" (including people) for support, so their emphasis on the individual's personal life history of internalized objects is another good conceptualization from which to search for core images.

Using both object relations theory and family systems theory, Merle Jordan adds a pastoral counseling focus by speaking of making "covenants with idols." By this he means an individual's distorted or false perceptions of ultimate authority in the "objects" or the false, limiting beliefs passed down through the generations in families. These are covenants made with less-than-ultimate objects and beliefs and thus cannot set us free, as a covenant with the true God can do. Jordan also points out that the emotion of guilt is felt by a person who tries to break free of such idolatrous covenants. By religious teaching, of course, the guilt should instead be felt for having the false god, not for breaking a false covenant.[11] What Jordan calls covenants with idols are also core images in the symbolic approach presented here.

Heinz Kohut's self psychology works with core images. This theory says that pathology comes when there is a chronic failure of the surroundings to reflect back to an individual that person's self, so that the development of the true self is hindered and becomes prone to fragmentation. Given the proper social psychological development, Kohut believes we are all equipped to mature into healthy, adult selves, so (though his theory rests on a psychoanalytic base) he falls within the "original blessing" school mentioned in chapter 6.[12]

Core images could be useful with Kohut's therapeutic analysis and method, which is a process of vicarious introspection which he calls "empathy," where the client is observed not only externally, but also listened to for what he viewed as an equally real factor, the meaning of the experiences for the person.

The "test" of whether a particular personality theory can be enhanced or helped by a core image and symbolic understanding is probably always in the practice: try it and see if it works.

Typologies

It will be apparent how I think most diagnostic systems work. I asked myself: if most psychological diagnostic systems lack precision, what do they have to offer us? I think the answer is that they are the typologies and structures we need. Certain basic universal tendencies can be identified, but—even more than with physiological descriptors—the diversity of human psychological functioning is far more striking than its unity. A theory of personality is at best a perspective which may prove helpful. Without ignoring either pathology or sin as true diagnostic observations of the human condition, we must always carefully keep all such structures as background.

For most of us, as I said before, the idea of "diagnosing" comes from the medical model of working with the body. When the body is ill, the doctor tries to diagnose where the illness lies and then from the store of learned medical knowledge prescribes a course of treatment to try to cure the illness. New discoveries are made all the time with the result that our medical knowledge has become vastly more efficient and capable of curing disorders which were formerly incurable.

The twentieth century has also vastly increased our knowledge of the psyche and how personality works. Disorders of personality have been studied, identified, and many times cured by various combinations of medical and psychological treatment. This is all to the good, except that psychological work, as I have suggested, must of its nature always be less precise than biophysiological work.

The discovery of a tumor with modern equipment is precise. Medical personnel can then make certain specific tests and say, for example, whether the discovered tumor is malignant or benign. A broken bone can be set with reasonable precision. Surgery can be performed to remove or repair or even replace diseased organs. These diagnoses and treatment plans are precise.

This model is not so well suited to matters of the psyche which are not solely based in biophysiology. Bodily development is more universal in pattern than psychic development; and disorders of the psyche, while some universal patterns or maps are obviously discoverable, cannot be diagnosed with anything like the same precision. Nor are treatment plans amenable to such precision. In fact, some of my medical friends tell me that even medical treatment is nothing like so precise as most lay people suppose. My obstetrician once educated me on this by saying, "Mrs. Clift, when any given doctor gives any given patient any given medicine, he really doesn't know what the effect will be. He only knows some odds." Medicine, too, especially in recent times sees beyond automatic health-and-sickness categories.

It is a vastly less specific knowledge even than the medical which we encounter in psychological problems, and the imprecision of medical-model diagnosis used in psychology has always seemed to me troublesome, and sometimes even dangerous. Much of my objection is met when we are clear that the categories are typologies.

The character disorders in the DSM III-R (the third edition of the *Diagnostic and Statistical Manual for Mental Disorders*, 1980), for example, are much more realistically viewed when they are seen as describing types than when they are seen as "mental disorders" in the sense of disease. I think it is important for counselors to be familiar with the general categories and some of the differential diagnoses in the DSM III-R, so long as we keep it in its place.

I can find the DSM III-R helpful as a typology. I think we all have tendencies toward some particular character disorder or to other kinds of disturbance. If we are going to get out of order, we will be likely to do it in a certain way. This view would see mental health and mental illness not as two separate kinds of entities, but as on a continuum, not discontinuous, as points along a spectrum—and not necessarily a rigid point either, so much as a movable point at different times in life. I think many therapists so view the DSM III-R, but I think when we do we are using it as a typology—as a general statement of types of behavior and response.

I also think, along with many modern professionals, that this and any other typology are most effectively used when the patient or client or directee, where possible, is enabled to make a self-diagnosis and take an active part in the movement toward health.

The Myers-Briggs Type Indicator (MBTI) is another typology, one which I use for aid in communication and to point the way toward which skills and skill areas are more difficult for each type person to develop. In that system, all the people in the world are characterized as one of sixteen different general types. It is helpful information. Yet the "indicator" is just that, and the literature about the MBTI urges readers to try out another type if their type description seems inaccurate.

These sixteen types are now further developed by subsets with additional scales, the Type Differentiation Indicator (TDI), which give even more information. Some theorists have also elaborated these sixteen types into additional "archetypes," as they call them— subsets which describe different ways of exercising one's type preference. There is a Jungian system of four different ways of being a woman, which another Jungian analyst has adapted to four different ways of being a man, and these can now be tested and identified in the usual manner of typologies.

The Enneagram is an increasingly popular typology which has nine types which give a different kind of information and which many people are finding quite helpful, both to identify their type of obsession and to point the way toward redemption of hurtful tendencies. The Enneagram goes beyond mere description of characteristics and "pierces through to the level of *motivation*" and thus serves as an "unfolding system of knowledge."[13]

The first typology I ever used was a little book by a German Roman Catholic spiritual director which used the earliest typology words I know of—the old Greek humors: choleric, sanguine, melancholic, and phlegmatic. There were more than four types, because he listed combinations of each of the four into subsets. These were related to the kinds of sins into which the different types of people were most likely to fall. My husband and I found this little book early in our marriage, and we were astounded to "find" ourselves there, along with some of the problems we had with each other.

There are dozens of other typologies and always have been. I have never yet read or heard about a typology which didn't give me some useful information. I think people are so complicated that they can be almost endlessly analyzed and categorized. The positive side of typologies is that we can see we are not alone; our tendencies which may seem so idiosyncratic are found in clusters in many people of our same type, and this can be a comfort and a help.

The downside is the resistance so many people have to any typology: I will not be put in a box. Actually, responsible typologies have no such intention and the literature says so at some length. If typologies are used to box people, they are being misused in a way that was never intended.

Yet there is an insidious pull toward this kind of boxing whether we are talking about a narcissistic personality disorder or an ESTJ or a #5 or a choleric or a Pisces. They are helpful, yes, some of them especially, but they are not, in a significant sense, *true*. This is an obvious statement, but one I think needs to be stressed— particularly with the diagnoses of the DSM III-R, where the pull is very strong to think that when we have made a diagnosis then we have said something final.

In my brief listing of typologies, I could also include the lists of qualities shared by Adult Children of Alcoholics, or Jung's theories of archetypes, or games people play. All of these are helpful, as are many other similar theory systems. They all have some empirical basis, relying on observation of numbers of people who share similar traits or behaviors.

What all of these systems share is that, like the typologies mentioned above, they are external to the individual client. Some lists of characteristics may be applicable and others may not. That is why all such responsible lists indicate that, say, any five of the following nine behaviors are sufficient for a diagnosis, or that many of the following twelve statements may be true of this diagnostic group.

I think Jung's analytical psychology intended originally to be free of systems, but it is not always so practiced. In the traditional Jungian model, personality can be understood in the general categories of mental disorders, but is not limited to them. Jung and his most careful followers never disdain using any theory of human personality which proves helpful in the work. They just think that "Psycho-pathology is redefined in terms of the symbolic content of its manifestations."[14] Yet even this individually focused theory can get lost if it begins to treat the archetypes as some kind of generalized diagnosis, giving this more importance than the individual's images.

As Jungians compile books of archetypes and books of the meaning of various symbols and books of mythology, they are all helpful. They are guides; they are typologies; we need to learn all we can about them. But as Joe Wheelwright says, we need to encounter the specific person before us and never let all this knowledge pour through the floodgates and get between us and the person we are working with. We need to scrub our cortexes clean. We need, as Jung says in another place, to learn all we can and then forget it when we face the person.

There are some general maps of the human territory, some of which lie in these typologies I have mentioned and in others. To enlarge our understanding of human personality, Jung suggests, in fact, that we study as maps the whole of human history, but especially the imaginal and sacred stories: ritual, myths, legends, stories, and fantasies (including "scientific" fantasies). At the same time, as general maps, they are not absolute; they are not necessarily *true* for the individual, just as other systems are not. The map is not the same thing as the territory; but at the same time you don't want to travel very far without a map.

From the developmental theories to the lists of games people play, these typologies are generalized, average observations which can be pointers for the therapist in diagnosing the particular problems or the particular level of development which the client needs to work on. They are ways of playing the odds. We need them to be part of our training, and most of us with experience select the particular ones which we use most consistently.

Yet I suggest that the primary diagnosis should be made with the client's life and material—narrative and core images—as the foreground. We can also make diagnoses according to the medical model or the spiritual direction model or whatever typology we know well enough to use, but the place of all such structural theorizing is decidedly in the background of the work. The helping professional then goes back and forth between this knowledge base and the concrete situation of the person or persons before us. Yet always the individual person—not individual psychodynamic theory, family systems theory, or psychosocial theory—must remain in the foreground, and somehow the individual focus must not be lost in the generalities of any structure.

This approach will also be significant, of course, in seeing how the diagnosis leads to the treatment plan. Essentially, the diagnosis and the treatment plan are intertwined—one leading inevitably to the other. So it is difficult to discuss one without the other. If the identified core images are indeed central to the client, they will begin to relate to one another. We are all probably clusters of core images, but these clusters will tie in with one another.

Even more significantly, they will point the way for healing, for change, for the continuing journey toward wholeness. Because they operate in genuine symbolic fashion, they will also carry in themselves the energy to help the journeying pilgrim continue the work with courage and imagination.

·8·

Treatment Planning

*E*ven more than providing the diagnosis, the core image leads to the treatment plan, whether we are "treating" ourselves in spiritual growth work or acting as a helper for others. The core image, in a mysterious way, contains the possibility of healing; the healing is inherent in the wound. The core images themselves carry within themselves the source of the recovery. They can become allies when they are befriended and lived with and let do their transforming work. Then we are not trying to fit our own or our client's lives into some norm or adjustment to culture as such, but to see where their lives need to go. To put it very simply, for example, if a client has little or no ego strength, the core image will be used to help build ego; if they have reached a place in life where it is time to sacrifice some of the outer ego-based life in order to deepen the inner life, the core image can point to an inner direction.

Beyond following the images where they point, there is nothing particularized or doctrinaire about how to work with core images that is different from other psychotherapeutic or spiritual direction methods, except the recognition of this genuine symbolic force for transformation. They give us clues to patterns which we can then work with in whatever methods we use.

As I discussed in chapter 6, "Operational Theory," this work does honor a transcendant component in transformation, beyond the mutual capabilities of both the client and the helper. Beyond any of the methods of work suggested hereafter, this overriding factor is to be remembered. Ultimately, the treatment plan of core image work comes from the images themselves.

This accords with the plea made to pastoral counselors and other therapists by the venerable Rollo May that psychotherapy must never be turned into mere techniques. Instead, he said, we must "deepen our sense of the mystery of human life." Without this basis we simply participate in the crisis of meaning which characterizes our age, and we ourselves burn out after a few years. To be genuinely helpful, May says we need to help people get to "touch, live with, achieve a connection with the deepest aspects of [their lives], with the mystery of it."[1]

This doesn't mean that he opposes techniques, nor do I. It simply means that techniques can never replace the complexity of human beings without the denial of their essential humanity. So it is with this transcendent position that symbolic work, including core images, begins, and by this basic position all methods are tested.

Association Experiment

To move from this transcendent plane to the level of clinical treatment plan, let me try to spell this out practically and then give some examples. I have already spoken several times about how we identify core images. Let me now make another connection.

We can look for the patterns that lead us to core images in a related way to the two kinds of definite symptoms Jung used in the association experiment. Jung evolved the association experiment early in his career. A list of key words is read by the tester to the client, and the client is asked to respond with the first word which comes to mind. The tester holds a stop watch and notes down both the word which the client gives in response and the time it takes to make the response.

Those responses and the times are then studied to find areas of disturbance. The theory is that when there is something unconscious which interferes with a normally timed response, the time lag will be longer, calling attention to the area of concern of the original test word. The responses themselves are also studied for clues to unusual connections. Disjunctions in either timing or ordinary associations can then be explored for clues to unconscious material. In fact, the association experiment was the first demonstrable proof of the existence of the unconscious which Freud and others had postulated.

It was also Jung's original basis for his theory of complexes, where he suggested that the association experiment showed the person's reaction to an actual inner conflict, found just as often among "normal" people. It was these problems and difficulties which brought his patients into disharmony with themselves that he identified as complexes.[2]

Working with Complexes

As I suggested in the chapter on diagnosis, there is a close relation between complexes and core images. The method of working with complexes is thus a helpful place to begin to work with core images.

Complexes are usually very old in us. They probably began, as I said, as a response which the child made to the world. A child's mind is incapable of discerning all the nuances of adult life, so children tend to make some emotional responses and judgments about themselves and the world which are the best they could do at the time.

I always tell people: don't knock your complex. You figured it out the best way you could with the material you had to work with. And it worked! You survived. It's just that as we get older complexes can outlive their usefulness for us. They can become the problem instead of the solution to the problem, as once they were.

This is when it becomes important to figure out where your complex areas are, because if you don't, they can keep whipping you around like a tail wagging a dog. You may *feel* very certain you are right, but really you are just in the grasp of your complex. So you work to know your complex areas; you *name* them. The so-called primitive cultures of the world have always known that we get some power over that which we can name.

What you can do with complexes once they are identified is use the knowledge to interpret the feelings, so they can be redone. For example, though in fact you feel like a helpless five-year-old girl, as once you were, you are no longer a helpless five-year-old girl. The complex brings up the same old feeling, and you feel helpless, like the little girl who felt "Stupie," even as a grown woman. But once a complex is named and identified, you can say to yourself: I was helpless then, but I'm not anymore, though I still feel that way. The feeling comes from the complex, not from present reality.

Once they are named then you know to be cautious. You know the areas where "you are not always right." You know the areas in which you need to exercise cautious discernment to test your emotional response. You can recognize the areas where you cannot trust your emotions to be giving you accurate information, where you need some other reality check than your emotional response.

As Jung has noted, "Everything that is highly toned is rather difficult to handle." We have physical reactions which cannot be easily brushed away.[3] When the complex becomes conscious, however, we feel an increase of personal power, a feeling of release and often of healing.[4]

A complex in one sense never goes away, because there may always be a tendency toward it, but it won't be with the same force. Eventually it may only come when you are tired, or stressed out, or sick, or don't eat. But even if it always comes back, it never has the same power after it is named. It cannot possess you in the same unconscious way. It is as if you have a new pair of corrective glasses to see your own responses more clearly.

I had an experience like this when I met with the cathedral staff to plan my ordination. I told them what I wanted—the hymns, the anthems, the people to present, the lay people and clergy to take various parts. They could not have been nicer, and I left and walked down the steps and suddenly realized that I was fighting to keep from crying. I thought: what is that about?

Then I remembered that, like so many women in our culture, I have a complex, an emotionally toned cluster of habitual response, about claiming my authority. It did not seem OK to me to ask for what I wanted—even at my own ordination. That is how I *felt*, but it wasn't true at all. And, furthermore, no one else but me even had the thought. When I cautiously checked it out, the other people on the staff never thought in any way that my asking for the hymns I wanted at my ordination was inappropriate. I felt it, but it was a distortion, and complex theory gives us a way of understanding these distortions.

It is important for all of us to know our complexes; but if you are working with other people, it is crucial. If you don't know your own, you will see your own in projection in everyone else.

You will know the areas where you need to be cautious. Just as I knew that I needed to check my feeling reaction against reality with extra care in claiming the authority to plan my ordination, you will know that you need to use extra care in thinking that other people have problems in your complex area.

Working with Core Images

The general pattern of the symbolic work with core images is like work with complexes. First, we must find the core images and name them. The intensity of the feeling in a given area is what usually leads us there, and the ruling categories of working with them are intensity and association. There is frequently an instantaneous recognition that something important is being seen. In each case the core image can be named by its shape, its contour, its gestalt, but one thing that calls attention to it is the level of emotion attached—either to the suffering which has been experienced or to the relief from the suffering.

Patterns of core images, like the areas of disturbance in the association experiment, are traced not only by the emotions around the image but also by a disjunction—a response which is not one to be expected. The emotion and/or the disjunction can be found around images which appear in any of the ways I have been suggesting, but one or both of them will probably be present to show that they are core images to the client, including being images of their particular delusional systems.

Secondly, when the charge of emotion comes (or the disjunction is noted), having named our core images, we can recognize that the emotional response lies in the area of the image. Then we know where the emotion or disjunction comes from. This has two important consequences. We don't blame ourselves or feel guilty for having the emotion or for our lack of logical associations, *and* we don't trust the emotion to be giving us true information. We are no longer so absolutely certain we are right. We know we need to check ourselves against objective reality.

Naming the core images and staying in relation to them give us the ability to do the reality checking and discernment and then to do the slow, steady work of redoing our view of the world and ourselves. This is the basic work of the symbolic journey and the basic work that counselors do probably most of the day, no matter what theoretical construct they use. It is inherent in the basic kind of listening stance, whether we are listening to our own inner reality or to the images from someone else's life.

The connection with true symbols also makes the reality present and it will continue to make it present when the work goes on. In fact, an interesting thing happens between you and the person you work with in core image work. The work takes over. There is a mutuality which can be stunning to therapists who are accustomed to slogging along trying to encourage clients to become more responsible.

I have been told by other therapists that this approach profoundly affected their work, that they began to look at their caseload in a whole new way and found it especially helpful in getting to the root things faster. One counselor felt that what "core image" gave her was a language to describe something familiar.

If our images are ignored, they will become more insistent until they carry us along to consciousness of the reality they assert. When we push core image patterns down into the unconscious, they don't simply go away. Rather, they stay down there, gathering energy and getting ready to burst out unexpectedly. Jung called this process by its classical name *enantiodromia*—the regulative function of the opposites where a consciously held view which becomes too extreme has a tendency to turn into its opposite. This is where the naming of the core images is crucial. No matter how bad the news is of one's inner shadow possibilities, it is better to know it than not to know it. It is in the knowing that the ability to overcome lies. One who will not face the shadow within will not grow toward more maturity.

Though I have done little of it myself, I think core image work can be done in groups. When I began lecturing on core images, people repeatedly told me they could resonate with the core images of other people they heard about. Furthermore, in hearing about others, they could actually experience healing themselves. Group work is an important modality in our alienated culture, so I hope this gets developed.

I have given a number of examples in Part I of places where core images can be found. These are intended to be suggestive for the counselor or spiritual director as places to take special care to listen for them attentively.

The counselor listens, for example, for one or maybe more than one incident from the client's life which are paradigmatic incidents—scenes which are formative. Such an example is Laura, the woman who tapes up her own mouth, a paradigm or picture of how she behaves in life. This picture-image sheds light on understanding how she functions. The image itself points to taking the tape off her mouth as the way of healing.

A more accurate way of speaking would be to say, "It is *as if* the tape is on her mouth." Truly, there is no tape, of course, except in her own fears and attempts to please and thus protect herself. This "as if" quality in the image is especially useful to point the way to the possibility of change. We really know that "the tape is on her mouth" *means* "she can take the tape off her mouth."

In the same way, to see that *Clarinda* always taught a moral lesson really *means* that the woman who remembered Clarinda can free herself from this manipulation by focusing on the escape into the free world her memory rejoiced in, not simply learning the manipulative moral lesson of obedience to parental authority. In the freed world of genuine adulthood, she can make her own decisions—joyfully.

The pastoral counselor who dreamed of the cathedral with foundations to the center of the earth can accept this image as his own and claim the peace which the dream brought him. His cathedral is deep within himself and will not be destroyed by changes in his religious affiliation. The cathedral within *means* he can move in the outer world without losing his own foundation. It is the "rock" upon which he can build his life.

Diane can look at her very negative core image of guilt for "bloody Jesus on the cross" and see that she did not cause the death. She only felt "as if" she did. Seeing this, she can move on to new images of the meaning of that bloody sacrifice on the cross, far beyond her personal, child's appropriation of guilt. "The life of every creature is the blood of it," says Leviticus (17:14). The blood points to life as well as death. By the power of her ritual and subsequent reflection and insight she can move beyond that personal, inflated guilt. She can see, through her personal ritual image of women's menstruation, the possibility of new life, and she can see through Good Friday to Easter. She can be a responsible adult without doing eternal penance which destroys her living spirit.

"As if" always includes the possibility of change, and thus in itself carries the hope which is the necessity of all psychotherapy. The "as if" image holds past, present, and possible future together, and by doing so points the way to its own transformative potential.

The case of Cathy who dreamed of the two snakes fighting illustrates how such a core image in a dream can continue to be useful for years. Three years after her fiancé's death, Cathy realized that the fighting snakes were pictures of the lifelong battle at the core of herself. By that time the core battle had shifted some and her own confidence was growing, but she wanted to return to therapy to work it through at a deeper level, beyond her original grief work.

She had done more inner self-examination, and she realized that, ever since she was quite small, she had felt inadequate with part of herself. There was always a negative voice in her head, claiming that she was worthless and incapable of achieving. Her very competitive family and demanding father whom she always wanted to impress were part of the background to these voices.

This can be expressed in many diagnostic forms. We could speak of the negative animus voices and her need to overcome their harmful effect in her life. We could analyze her situation in family systems terms, placing her in the context of the different family roles she, her siblings, and her parents filled. We could point to the social significance of the culture in which she was brought up, where women were relegated to certain limited roles, so that the loss of her fiancé was equal to the loss of purpose in her life.

Each of these methods of making a treatment plan for working with Cathy would be helpful, but I suggest that they are helpful as background and that as a foreground to all these generalized, systemic theories, the most helpful method of all is to go to the core image her dream has presented. This is the tailor-made picture of her battle, and its energy can continue to inform her and point the way to her personal life transformation. It is *as if* a snake is on her side, a snake that is like her admired sister Mary. Cathy herself in the dream was on the side of the Mary-snake and she could see that it might win. This helped to create hope in her and gave her a dream image that she could continue to use for her own lifetime fight to transcend her depressive snake.

With luck and more differentiation, the inner battle may move into more conscious, human forms. She may be able to choose the creative side of her snake-battle, incident by incident, with increasing insight and confidence. When that is achieved sufficiently, her images may begin to change. The counselor can be ready to identify this new form of the ally that appears in the dream as the Mary-snake.

This is how images can help us toward *life*. Images may help to figure out what is blocking us from life. Images can help life be transformed. Sometimes we can use core images as the images of our power and intentionally take these strong image-symbols like the Mary-snake with us when us go into a difficult situation in which we feel threatened.

So, as a counselor working with a frightened person, you stay on the lookout for the parts of themselves which can be your allies. This individualized system of order contains teleological possibility for their healing.

One such core image was there for me in an unexpected place in the initial history I took from a competent, successful, professional woman. As a part of my History Form, I ask for an Educational History. She laughed when I asked and told me she had been to twenty-two different schools by the time she graduated from high school. She said, "Once I stayed in a school almost a year." She treated this at the time almost as a joke, blithely commenting that it was a real training school to be in a regular army family and have to make a place for yourself in so many new schools. She had disavowed the emotional importance of this repeated experience; the image of her moving so much had no affective connection for her.

Further into the therapy, this life experience became a way of describing how she met life, which could be expressed this way: all life is a test, and she's always in a new school. She connected it with her continuing anxiety that she was never quite up to par, that she was never quite going to "pass" the test of life. Putting it in the context of her life "training" gave her a perspective from which to understand the sudden, irrational worry, what she called "senseless agitation," which could grab her at any moment. She could then both appreciate why she felt worried and move beyond the generalized worry into whatever specific fear she was facing. The emotional impact, thus understood, was put into a new/old perspective. It is slow work, needing to be done over and over, but she had a handle on how to do the work herself.

Another way to describe this relation between core images and treatment plan would be to say that you respect and follow the clients and their material. You wait on the unconscious. The core images of each life contain possibilities of healing and possibilities of destructiveness. At every step of life, we can go either way. It is in this tension of choice that therapy can be done with the images.

I think that following the client's material also gives the counselor the appropriate timing to focus on a given area of work. The personal material is followed and interventions offered on the basis of the unconscious hints from the client's material. It takes away some of our strain as helpers. We can offer and then set free. We can let plateaus come, work on the healing that is possible, and wait for another time when the person is ready for more.

The symbolic path is sometimes painfully slow, but, as Marie-Louise von Franz has observed: "If one watches this meandering design over a long period of time, one can observe a sort of hidden regulating or directing tendency at work, creating a slow, imperceptible process of psychic growth—the process of individuation."[5]

The patience needed for this process is also emphasized in spiritual development literature. There the ultimate direction is from the Holy Spirit; the organizing center of each life is God. The striving without ceasing which is recommended in scripture is a cooperative venture between the individual and God. As Alan Jones has said, "[H]uman beings don't just happen," and he adds: "We are made and re-made. In fact our becoming fully human depends on our willingness to respond to God's challenge to us to be more than we think we are."[6]

It takes real courage for genuine growth, and no one of us can know what is courage for another. Courage doesn't consist in doing something which is hard for another person, but in doing what is hard for you. When the dynamics of the unconscious are liberated, it takes courage to face all that of which we are ashamed, all the conflicts within us, all that holds us back from becoming what we are to be and thus doing what we are to do. The dreams and other symbolic representations will lead both counselor and client at the speed that is possible to the client.

If the client is courageous and continues to work, the images will connect the person to her or his own truths. Once the images are identified and worked with to deeper insights, the client has a continuing tool to work with after therapy, so the growth process can continue. The process is thus given back to the client—the whole purpose of the work toward healing and wholeness. As von Franz puts it, "The purpose of the work is to release you to the care of the eternal analyst within."

Helpful Methods of Symbolic Work

I have mentioned a number of ways in the preceding material that core images can be worked with. Most of the methods of intervention or self-help which we have learned in the process of personal growth or training can be used with this symbolic understanding; many of us have probably used symbolic approaches.

Earlier, I made a rough division of symbolic work into two general categories: interpretive and experiential. Sometimes a method of working with images moves back and forth between the two, and this combination may be the most helpful of all. Let me mention some of the modes I have found most consonant with symbolic work.

Interpretation of Symbols

Interpretation of symbols is a way of striving for insight and understanding. Partly the need for such understanding may be of special importance for particular types of people, but any type may find that their energy is freely released only when they can understand themselves and their processes. I think here of the woman who dreamed of the wedding garment and was only released from her twenty years of worry over the dream when she came to a new understanding of its meaning. Experience of God's love, even in very personal ways, had not released the worry until she understood.

Other times interpretation without experience can prove to be a blind alley for healing and wholeness. Understanding can be merely an intellectual exercise without achieving true changes in the person. They can be spoken of as "keeping it all in their heads." In such a case, then, some of the experiential modes of work are called for in order to bring the understanding home to the whole person. Memory generally, though, can lead to important understanding. If as Frederick Buechner said, "[E]verything that ever was continues not just to be, but to grow and change with the life that is in it still," then understanding our images can lead us toward seeing how they might change in our lives. We can see these possibilities as we make a thoughtful application of the core images to all the events of our lives.

Understanding at its most basic involves making the connections through the core images with our personal themes and patterns. As we see these connections, we tune into the movement and rhythm of our lives and begin to be able to imagine transcending whatever stasis or stuck place we are caught in. Even if the core image is very negative in its effect on us, it points to healing by seeing what its opposite would be.

One of the best aids to memory and to finding our personal patterns comes from making a family genogram. This is a kind of elaborated family tree that records not only the usual birth-marriage-death information, but more personal information about lives and relationships over several generations. Because we can then see the family laid out, we may spot patterns that are not so apparent without this graphic context. Genograms can thus be a rich resource for insight and understanding.[7]

The discernment involved in checking our own reactions and opinions against objective reality is always an aid to insight. Understanding the source of our own distortions is also a help in moving beyond them. If a core image comes from early childhood, our distortions can be seen more clearly when we go over them from the adult perspective on their meaning in contrast to the child's view, as when the woman who loved *Clarinda* as a child and experienced it then as escape literature realized as an adult that it had defined her childhood prison of compliance.

Insight is also gained from realizing what choices are available to us; in and of itself this moves beyond experienced or feared limitations. Sometimes insight can come simply from seeing that the core image has more than one possible meaning, as when Linda Leonard connected the hellfire of addictive craving with her creative fire. Writing can be an aid to insight. Something about the objectification of personal material by getting it out of ourselves and onto paper helps us see it more clearly. Some of the narrative and journaling techniques also involve the experiential, and I will refer to those again below, but the use of words tends toward the analytic and interpretative as well.

Poetry as a particular kind of writing can be a good way to get a handle on insight and understanding. Earlier in my life when I was working through a depression, someone gave me a little book of Japanese haiku poems in translation. These are small, three-line poems whose form is ruled by the number of syllables in each line: five in the first line, seven in the second, and five in the third. I found myself beginning to think in that rhythm, and in a matter of a few months had written dozens of them.

That was the first time I began to realize the therapeutic value of writing poetry. As I said, only half facetiously, "If I can get something into seventeen syllables, I can handle it." I was regaining confidence in my own ability to deal with life, much as a child experiences in nondirective play therapy, but I was doing so in part because I had not only the control inherent in the poetry line and the emotive effect of poetry, but also the cognitive insight into meaning which this combination enabled.

Amplification of images is also of continuing help in interpreting them—not only personal amplifications, but the general ideas that come from whatever knowledge we have of mythology, religion, history, folklore, anthropology, zoology, literature, fairy tales, and the general body of human knowledge. None of us is conversant with all these areas, but we all have areas of knowledge we can call on to suggest general amplification. If we keep strongly in mind the strictures against reifying symbols, good symbol dictionaries can be an aid.[8]

Lastly, of course, all the specialized body of knowledge about human personality and functioning which I have placed in the background in my chapter on diagnosis is helpful. If used in its proper background place, any of that information is helpful amplification of our particular core images and patterns.

Experiential Work

As I said above, some methods of work overlap both interpretative and experiential, but generally speaking, experiential work is that which tries to bring the image into the feeling life—the part of symbolic work which stresses carrying the feeling forward, even without necessarily understanding what it means. In fact, most therapists think that healing cannot occur unless some emotional impact is involved beyond cognitive understanding and insight.

Sometimes this emotional involvement follows on the heels of insight, but sometimes there is a need for intentional experiential encouragement in order to bring the change deeply into our beings. It is thus possible to use a core image to help bring about change without new insight. In short term therapy, for instance, a core image can be a referent point to reframe the image or to challenge or encourage changed behavior. Empathic mirroring of one's personhood is itself an experiential change-bringer.

One excellent experiential method for working with images involves reentering the image imaginatively, or "dreaming it on" to see where it leads you. This is the process Jung called "active imagination" to distinguish it from passive daydreaming. Several books suggest how one can be helped with active imagination in all its myriad forms; Robert Johnson's *Inner Work* is a good "how to" book on this feeling way.[9]

Probably the most thorough and helpful model for doing active imagination is the kind of journaling that Ira Progoff's Intensive Journal Workshops teach. Progoff did his doctoral thesis on Jung, and then while he was at Drew University, he and his students did research on creative people, trying to discover what makes people creative. Their primary discovery was that the continuing contact or dialogue between consciousness and the unconscious was the source of creativity. From this beginning place, he explored ways to open up that dialogue, and these are taught in his journaling books and in the workshops.

This is far beyond any simple diary writing, because its whole purpose is to open up the dialogue between consciousness and the unconscious so that the possibilities for growth locked away in us can be freed. This way of working begins experientially, but, despite Progoff's strictures against interpretation, it also leads to insight and understanding. It does, however, have the symbolic gift of carrying us forward on the energy unloosed by the journal processes.[10]

I discovered an interesting aspect of this kind of inner narration while preparing this book for publication. Some of the people who gave me their stories for this book had written them for me, but others I had interviewed. So I sent them the results of my write-up of the interviews to make sure their story was accurately expressed. They had almost a universal response to the first reading—being moved, frequently to tears. They tended to put it aside and then go back for subsequent readings later. The second readings evoked responses such as one man, who said, "It is as if I have longed for years for someone to tell my story, and it is wonderful." The experience of seeing the core image traced, in writing, was deeply healing.

Some kinds of prayer, such as meditation, contemplation, and contemplative prayer, have long been ways of touching deeply into an experiential place in the practitioner. Continued practice of such meditative or contemplative prayer is reported to increase the experience of change. The most prominent contemporary teacher is the Trappist monk Thomas Keating, whose contemplative prayer outreach introduces many to this practice.

Many theorists encourage and teach ways of getting in touch with feelings, from the spiritual exercises of St. Ignatius onward; this is especially important in modern culture which has tended to intellectualize life and dishonor emotions. Among the most popular psychological approaches has been John Bradshaw's work. He and others have urged us to feel the pain of our inner child, who still lives within each of us, in order to work beyond that pain instead of staying trapped in it. Frequently such work involves connecting with games or toys or stuffed animals such as a child might enjoy. It is almost as if the process of development through relating to transitional objects is reversed by the adult to get back to the child's feelings.

A step beyond getting in touch with feelings is the way Gene Gendlin describes his method, called "focusing," which he thinks is a natural internal process of harnessing our body's wisdom. Focusing is a step-by-step process, clearly outlined by Gendlin, where a particular problem is focused on intentionally. Then you try to sense what your body feels when the problem is focused on. The quality of that "felt sense" is contemplated until a word or phrase comes to mind out of the felt sense. Then the person goes back and forth until the body gives an answer or a new solution comes, which Gendlin says, "feels like a relief and a coming alive."[11] In her introduction to his book, Marilyn Ferguson equates what Gendlin calls the "body" with the "deeper, wiser self" in each of us. Whatever language or metaphor you prefer, this process is based on an optimistic view of the healing power in the individual in terms of process instead of pathology, and as such it is a very useful one for core image work.

Many kinds of body work are available for help in experiencing our images. One of the most fruitful is dancing or acting it out. Working in different chairs to dialogue with a different part of oneself can evoke change. Reentering the power of an image with our bodies as well as our minds and imaginations can bring home the power of the image in a whole new way.

Similarly, various art forms can give us a different relationship with our core images—painting, drawing, sculpting. This also gives us an objective picture of the image from which we can continue to learn. Sand box work, play therapy, storytelling, and other similar techniques accomplish the same kind of healing.

Some group work, such as psychodrama, role play, Gestalt dream work, or family sculpting, have a similar emotive power which not only touches into the old feelings about the image, but also carries the image forward. Most family systems theorists work toward experiential change by focusing on processes in the family as being more significant than content.[12] Yet, as I have said, I think the family patterns themselves can be understood as core images by systems theorists working with families as well as individuals.

Rituals of various kinds, either traditional ones or rituals which arise out of the individual person, speak to a deeper than conscious level of the personality whenever a genuine connection is made between person and ritual. Ritual can then be a transforming experience in and of itself; it has a creative potential for generating change, to make new.[13] Frequently, a person seems not to *know* in a felt sense that something is changed until there is a ritual acting out the change.

Such rituals can be very simple and individual, such as one reported by Robert Johnson, of a man who ritually affirmed his work to overcome a life pattern with junk food by buying and burying the biggest deluxe cheeseburger and fries—with "high, solemn ceremony." For him this was a "symbolic act of renunciation" including all that the use of junk food symbolized in his life.[14]

Ritual action taken within traditional religious patterns or services may work well here, or traditional religious forms can be claimed and practiced in such ways as confessing to another person and then burning the list of confessed material ritually. Sometimes rather formal rituals can be written and then experienced, either alone or with others.

An example of a creative ritual response to a life memory is one prepared for herself by a survivor of childhood parental suicide. This survivor is a psychotherapist and a minister. Because she is trained in liturgy and ceremonial, she was able to prepare her own healing ritual and at the same time take her readers through the process of preparing their rituals. It thus becomes a helpful treatment model for other wounds as well.[15]

Finally, of course, many techniques of traditional psychotherapy are working at the felt-sense level. Mirroring reflection, for instance, by the therapist can change a client's experience of herself or himself without any cognitive interpretation. Various modalities from theories as varied as primal scream therapists and healing-of-the-memories prayers all operate from experiential methods and can help change our images toward our healing and wholeness.

·9·

Working Through Case Material

*T*his chapter explores how core images can guide the work of a lifetime, ever revealing new directions and depths, until the tapestry of a life is woven from the continuing threads of the images. To do this, I have chosen two more lengthy case studies of following core images where they lead. Both these people have had some therapy help and some spiritual direction, but most of the continuing work with the core images is the search by the people themselves. The focus here is thus on the way in which symbolic work with primary images continues to be available for bringing light and direction to the journey of life.

The first case covers a period of about five or six years; the second a period of thirty-five years. Over time the enlightenment from the beginning core images includes areas and nuances not suspected in the beginning. Both used a number of sources, found additional images which interacted with the first, and employed several of the techniques mentioned in the last chapter—always attempting, as Rollo May urged, to achieve a connection with the deepest aspects of their lives, with its mystery.

The Goat and the Train

The first case I have chosen is that of Steve from chapter 4. Steve, you will remember, is the young minister whose core image initially came to him from a folk song he had learned to play on the piano as a child, "Bill Grogan's Goat." We left him there having analyzed some of the interactions with his family of origin where he had come to play the scapegoat and also having found work which fulfilled his personal sense of vocation to inner spiritual work.

The concept of the scapegoat comes from an annual atonement ritual in ancient Israel outlined in Leviticus. The priest would present two goats, one of which was sacrificed; the other was the scapegoat. The priest confessed the sins of Israel over the scapegoat, which was then driven into the wilderness, carrying off the sins of the nation.

Family systems therapists consider the "identified patient" in a family to be analogous to the scapegoat. That family member is the one held responsible for the family problem, thus relieving the rest of the family of their guilt and conflict. "By being the family's burden bearer and the focus for conflict, the scapegoat seeks to secure atonement for the family by being its sacrificial lamb."[1]

Steve, as the one who broke mom's leg, the one characterized by his sister as "a mistake from the beginning," and the Dagwood of the family, learned early to fill the scapegoat role. As an adult he continued the pattern, especially in the goat role of associate pastor. He drove himself out (with a little help from the denominational executives) into the wilderness of unemployment and the actual wilderness of an unheated rural cabin.

For further development of Steve's story, I will quote his own words much of the time, with a few of my interpretations added.

When I first called Steve about using his core image of "Bill Grogan's Goat" for this book, he was interested in pursuing its meaning, and we made an appointment to talk about it. After the phone call he played around with the song itself and the images in it, and then the night before our appointment he had a dream. He said when we met that he had remembered so few dreams for several years that the fact that he had this dream the night before our meeting was significant and felt like "a bit of a gift for us today." This was his dream:

> I was in a wheelchair in a school, and my teacher came to me also in a wheelchair—a man. Dream ego recognized him. In other words, there was a bond or a relationship, but I didn't recognize him. And he said something to the effect that I could

be readmitted to class by writing a newspaper article on my injury.

At some point of the dream I realized that my injury was around my ankles. There was some kind of injury there or weakness, but I could propel myself in the wheelchair with my feet. In other words, I could kind of walk myself, and so I headed toward the classroom down this long hall, and I rolled down a kind of graceful slope in this hall toward where the class room door was. And as I got to the door, so did the teacher also roll down. He went on into the classroom and kind of disappeared at that point into the class, which was full of people. And I went through the door and just inside and could not find enough space or a comfortable place. There was a girl to my left, a young woman, and I kind of said "Excuse me," you know, asking her to get out of my way so that I could get around and find a place. And that was it.

We both connected our planned interview with the dream image of working on the newspaper article, or as Steve put it, "like a succinct report on the pattern or the cycle that the song describes, of my emotional programming—the false self system, so it's kind of a succinct summary of that."

He was also interested in the focus on the ankles, because the goat in the song in his imagination is tied by the ankles. So he felt that "the bond or the bind, the attachment, the fixation, the compulsion, whatever, is there." The injury to his ankles was like an image of the helplessness he felt so often.

Yet the dream suggests that if he will work on his "newspaper article," he can get back in class—learn something more and find a place in the classroom of life.

Steve had been gathering information for his "newspaper article." Among other things, his wife had found another version of "Bill Grogan's Goat" for him, and this version had several different emphases. Folk songs, of course, have many varieties of the same song, all from a general originating structure.

The new version starts with the love a man had for his goat:

> He loved that goat,
> Indeed he did,
> He loved that goat,

Just like a kid.

One day that goat
Felt frisk and fine
Ate three red shirts
Right off the line.

The man, he grabbed
Him by the back
And tied him to
A railroad track.

This version also continues with the goat in fright coughing up
the shirts and flagging the train. Steve felt this version also caught
a dynamic in his family relationship—especially with his father. He
described it like this:

> And it is like when I'm feeling fine or euphoric, free and great,
> something comes along that flattens that affect, destroys it. And
> it's as if I put myself in relationships that maintain that.
>
> That's something I remember from my childhood. When I
> was free, big, feeling expansive, in my element, my Dad would
> come home, find something to get angry at and spank me. And
> it got to the point where if he would come in the house and
> bang the door closed, I'd run downstairs and clean my room up,
> because I knew he'd come down and get mad because my room
> was a mess and punish me.
>
> Now the dream says, in a situation of entering back into class,
> the teacher is there—both in wheelchairs. My admission back
> into the next lesson is to put this in summary form, in newspaper
> form, so that it becomes history, to bring closure to it and let it
> go and go on. So it's as if I'm processing closure and articulation.
> This is a part of the letting go of those blocks.

I think it's also interesting that Steve was attracted to this second
version of the song, because, despite the dangerous act of tying the
goat to the railroad track, there is the initial emphasis on the fact
that the man "loved that goat, just like a kid." My sense of Steve's
relationship to his family was that, even in their dysfunction, he
experienced love.

Almost casually, Steve added another, contemporary incident, which I think also resonated with the dream imagery:

> I've been aware for a while that when I'm around people—I get blamed for things I have nothing to do with. How am I responsible?
> I was aware that somehow, in forming relationships, that theme was there, but what blew my mind recently was: a young man in a wheelchair [Joe], whom I scarcely knew. I was standing in the office area, and he was near me. I was in conversation with someone else, and somebody dropped something, and he looked at me and said, "That was your fault, you know."
> And I thought: how does this work? This person and I have had such minimal contact that this attitude is not being consciously transmitted, and yet he articulates this script as if he were a part of my family.
> I'm at the place in my journey where I'm the most conscious of not giving myself to these things. I'm in a really good place, and I'm not consciously giving myself to this trap, and it goes on anyway. And it's like I stand by my false-self system, and it runs itself. There's a kind of horror to that. This man I hardly know is playing my script, and I'm not involved in it.

One connection at least that we can see is with the two men in wheelchairs in the dream. Steve himself is like Joe, the man in the wheelchair in outer life who blames Steve for no apparent reason. He has internalized that blaming attitude, and it hampers him in life. Yet his "teacher" is also in a wheelchair, so somehow the class and the newspaper article can teach him something new about his "disability."

Steve then told me of another connection he had made. As I mentioned in chapter 4, he had another core image song, also about trains. This was a folk song based on an American hero, Casey Jones. Steve's dad told him that when he was about six he had a record of "Casey Jones" that he played daily on his phonograph. Steve couldn't remember the song, but he told the story of the song's narrative with gusto:

> My other myth is Casey Jones. That's a humanization, in a sense, of this savior figure. The story I know. He was a tremendous American hero figure. He was a young engineer; he had a

wife and a kid or two, I guess. He had this great reputation on the Illinois Central for always being on time. One of his buddies got sick, and he had to take a double shift, and the train was behind schedule. He was the engineer and had a black man firing the coal. They were trying to make up time.

He was doing a hundred miles an hour on the straightaway at one point between two towns in Illinois on a passenger run. The people loved him and could tell it was Casey Jones by the way he tooted the whistle in all the farm lands around there. He was making up time, but safety was his first goal.

I'll interrupt Steve's story briefly here to comment that "safety" being Casey Jones's first goal seems a little thin to me. Doing a hundred miles an hour on a straightaway trying to make up time on a passenger run doesn't sound like safety to me. I think that is an interpolation of Steve's. To continue his story:

He sees a caboose light ahead in a place it's not supposed to be. It's foggy and rainy. He starts to apply the brakes and tells his fireman to jump because they're going to crash, and he manages to slow the train down so much that when the collision hits, he's the only one who is killed. No one else is killed. And the legend is that when they found him, he was still in the driver's seat with the throttle in his hand.

I started to play that story out as a child. I'd build cardboard trains in the back yard, and I'd spend hours. For me this was meditation. I would go into an interior place of total absorption. I would enact this.

Then I had model trains. Then I built live steam locomotives—each about four feet long—and I know how they operate—the nuts and bolts. And I live in [an old railroad town].

The whole fact is that instead of being the goat, Casey Jones was the engineer. He was in control of the train. He gave his life. The goat had no capacity. He's a Jesus figure, because he saw a situation where death was impending, and he was able to make choices, even though they were sacrificial and difficult choices, to give his life for the common good.

That's what I did at the church where I was the associate. In the earlier two [job crises in my life], I was the goat, just going through the instinctual, collective process. But something happened there. Well, I lost the position, but something happened. I had moved from being the goat, I think, to being Casey Jones.

I brought that collision course to a reasonably safe conclusion.
I gave my life [chuckle]. I was in utter humiliation.
So I just coughed up the flag.

Steve also said that before he began to explore new ways he had
felt tied to the wheel of life—like the Lionel trains he had as a child,
going round and round the Christmas tree and getting nowhere.
The new ways included his study of contemplative prayer, mentioned in chapter 4. You will remember that Steve had felt called to
a ministry of inner work and spiritual direction, but found no place
to exercise this sense of vocation in his church. When he lost his
position as associate of the church, he used his severance pay as a
sabbatical. He began to study mysticism, stayed in what he called
a "vacuum," and practiced centering prayer.

He learned his centering prayer through the ministry of Thomas
Keating, the Trappist monk who has a ministry of teaching this
form of prayer. Shortly after his acceptance by Thomas Keating
into his program, he had a wonderfully affirming initiation dream:

> I underwent an initiation ceremony into an Order to which
> Thomas Keating belonged. I felt strange and guilty because I
> knew I had a family and I couldn't "go all the way" with them,
> but the ceremony of inclusion into this community was so beau-
> tiful and moving, as they reclothed me, candles and wreath in
> my hair, new robe, prostrating before the chancel.

The dream affirms that Steve has at long last found his way to
carry out his sense of vocation to emphasize the inner journey,
even though his own religious tradition has no such specialized
vocation for the work. He borrows the forms from the Roman
Catholic tradition, and they welcome him into their community.
He was off the railroad track and onto the track of his calling.

Eventually he was called as pastor of a wonderful little mountain
church which needed someone part-time, and he became a teacher
and team member of a centering prayer group. At the time of
our interview he reported that the work he was in felt completely
different to him from any work he had ever been in.

At the same time, he could see that the possibility of repeating
his old patterns was present when he went to his new church,
which I will call Mountain Town. By the time he went there, he

had new colleagues with whom he could process his experiences. One of these, a woman I will call Carmel, was especially helpful. This was how he described the danger and overcoming it:

> Yes, but, there were markers. I think I could have made Mountain Town like the others. The mix was there. I learned through my work with my earlier therapist, my reading in family systems, and some of the other stuff that I could say to myself, "Yes, but this is different."
>
> So that when the emotional commentaries were going on, I could derail [!] some of that by saying, "Yes, but, this is different." Then I began to process the variables in a different way.
>
> Carmel was helpful in saying, "These people aren't blaming you for those people getting mad and leaving the church." She was there to point out things to me.
>
> Mountain Town is the way to come to a redemptive finish with the church. It's the first place I've wanted to stay and can say I love it.
>
> The first one and a half years were hell—mostly paranoia from past experience—no objective reality to that. As I relaxed into it with a supportive community, it was like I was in a different world. I don't want just to get out of that pattern, but to see my vocation. What is my vocation?
>
> In my inner work in the mystical dimension of consciousness, which I feel I'm accessing and able to articulate and even able to transmit, I feel like I am in my element, my role, my place. For the first time, I'm not looking ahead—down the track. I would like to stay where I am indefinitely. I'm happy in my work. I don't feel the compulsion I used to feel: constantly worrying what's going to happen next.
>
> Well, that's antithetical to contemplative prayer, which is living in the cloud of unknowing. That's healing for me. From Carmel and others, I have gotten that positive, life-giving, supportive, mirroring affirmation that I didn't receive as a child.
>
> This little goat swallows its power, but then in order to get free, regresses and finds the power again. The only problem with this story is that it doesn't end with the goat getting get off the tracks. It just ends with the goat stopping the train. A more fitting conclusion to me is getting off of the damn tracks.
>
> There's this sense of not using my person power initially that gets me into this position where it appears that I am the cause of the tension, so that I have to solve it. I cough up whatever

personal power I have, but it's not solved because of no consciousness. So I went through this three times. But something is happening that is different because I'm using my personal power.

The "three times" refer to three jobs Steve had at different times, the last of which was the associate pastor position previously discussed. All three had ended in "disaster" for him. It is interesting that fairy tales so frequently have three events before the final redemption, and, of course, Bill Grogan's goat ate three red shirts.

With his new insights he connected this trail of disaster with his family history. There was, first of all, the significant incident when he was three of his mother breaking her leg, when he later found she had miscarried. He realized, "My mother was not watching where she was going as we walked down the street. She was distracted by a shop, looking in the windows, and she fell over me and broke her leg." However, as mentioned in chapter 4, for most of his growing up years, the story was told, jokingly, by his father of how he broke his mother's leg. "I was the cause of that accident. And that was all the story that I knew until I began to process this stuff."

In fact, there were two miscarriages and a stillborn between Steve and his younger brother. He now thinks that part of his sense of causing accidents came from this family situation. He said, "Those lost babies might have tied me to this cycle. So there was a sense that I had taken somebody's life and in a sense I had to fill in their position or their role and was not free to live my own. I see that in the jobs that I would go into."

He could identify this motif in each of the jobs where he got in trouble with the authorities, "I wasn't filling the role. Same thing at [my old church]. The emotional system said you aren't doing your job, which is to complete the pastor, who is not functioning."

He also felt that another line from "Bill Grogan's Goat" had deep significance for him—"doomed to die." Some of his own spirituality had been built on an image of death—like a death fear or something during childhood, perhaps again related to the three lost babies and other accidents in his family.

He made two other associations at the time of our interview. He connected coughing up with Jonah—one who runs away from his call and one who brings bad luck or misfortune, both of which he had done or been perceived as doing by others. He said, "That's why they tossed Jonah overboard."

The other brought a rueful laugh, when he identified the locomotive, a kind of fire-breathing dragon, with his image of God.

After our interview, Steve called me with some more developments before this text went to press.

First, at a contemplative prayer training session, a memory from childhood had popped up—of being forced to go to swimming lessons. The instructor used humiliation to force pupils to jump off the diving board into deep water—a sink-or-swim philosophy. Steve hated the lessons with all his six-year-old heart; and when he checked with the other boys in his family who were forced to go, they had hated them too. None of them, even as adults, would let their parents minimize the pain of the experience.

Interestingly, the memory popped into his mind when he was feeling the same kind of force in some of the group process at the training session, where there was some expression of the opinion that people should learn contemplative prayer by just being "thrown in the water to sink or swim." His childhood memory of his hated swimming lessons gave him the courage to speak up to the group with his objection, and the group changed to what he called a "more humanizing way."

He also got a missing piece of family information on a visit—that in several generations of his family there had been a rather tragic or gruesome death of a child. His death fear had deeper roots than he had realized.

He also speculated that somewhere between six and nine, he himself had moved his core myth from "Casey Jones" to "Bill Grogan's Goat"—to a myth where he didn't have to die like Casey Jones did. His drive for life was reflected in the change of songs. Readers will perceive that this is a change in his original position that Casey Jones was a development beyond Bill Grogan's Goat. He had stayed open to wherever the images led him, even to reversing a former interpretation.

I suggested to him that, though Casey Jones was in fact a savior figure, he was also something of a *puer aeternus*—eternal boy. His racing down that track at a hundred miles an hour has that element of grandiosity in it, without control or limits. Though Steve began by thinking that Casey Jones was superior to Bill Grogan's goat, he had now reversed that opinion. Bill Grogan's goat could stop the train in time to avoid death.

The third new development was a dream he had where he came face to face with "himself." The "other" self was taller than he so that he had to look up to him. He was calmly getting ready, with plenty of time, relaxed and smiling.

This was the reverse of a common nightmare he had for years, where he was unprepared for worship, guilty and distracted, feeling "it's too late." His new dream began like that, but at the end he returned to his preparation, not anxious, and in control—the antithesis of his usual nightmare. An introvert, he had always had preparation anxiety and even panic at the thought of public humiliation if he didn't do a good job.

For him the new dream was like a capstone of his core image work, as well as all the other work he had done. It felt like a smiling blessing that he gave himself.

Illness and Betrayal

For another case example, I have written of my personal work over a period of thirty-five years with a core image of my own life—one of those which I am willing to share. I make this choice simply because it is the only one I have been able to follow for that long a period of time. The image I will trace begins with my flawed emotional response to illness.

My exploration of it began, as I see by hindsight, with one of my spiritual struggles after I became a practicing Christian as an adult. I was trying to reform my life and grow in the ways I thought a Christian should grow, but one of the nagging problems I continued to have would happen when anyone close to me got sick. I always had the same immediate irrational reaction: I was enraged at them.

I was ashamed of feeling this way, of course, so I hid it as best I could and tried to behave appropriately toward the sick person despite my inner feelings. I knew that it was wrong to feel anger at a person who really needed sympathy and nurture, so I experienced it as a failure in my Christian life. I confessed my guilt to God and asked for help to overcome my anger and become a nicer person. Looking back on it, I can't say that I focused on this particular failing more than others; there were a lot of things to work on, but it was a continuing area of experienced failure for me. It is interesting to note, however, that during those first ten years of my adult Christian life, I became quite interested in the healing ministry and began to work in that field.

When I went to Zurich to study at the Jung Institute in the mid-1960s, this problem eventually came up in the material, and I began to deal with it in my analysis. During my first year of analysis, I had a dream in which my parents were at my home with me. My father lay in bed, quite pale. My mother came in and whispered that he had a headache. Then he began to speak very softly, so that I could hardly hear, and my mother explained that he was saying what he wanted to eat for dinner. What he wanted was something that was totally unavailable—food from a restaurant two thousand miles away—but he felt that this was the only thing he could eat. Mother and I whispered back and forth softly, guessing what he might like to eat that we *could* get for him. We couldn't ask him because he only wanted the unavailable food. She cautioned me not to tell him what she had said he might want, but nevertheless just to try to please him. I offered him something that I could prepare, but he declined with a sigh.

My associations with the dream scene were several. Certainly my father had regular headaches all his life, as did most of his immediate family—the Dalbys "had headaches." When they did, everyone was expected to tiptoe around, and, generally speaking, the one with the headache must be catered to.

I also thought of a passage in C. S. Lewis's *Screwtape Letters* where Lewis discusses people who think they are undemanding because they ask for so little, but really they are quite demanding. They really demand that they have exactly what they want, however troublesome it is to others, while feeling that what they ask for is just so little.[2]

My analyst asked why I thought my father had headaches—what did they accomplish for him. What need of his did the headaches respond to? I thought a bit and then said that I thought they got him some time away by himself, without his having to ask for it. Then my analyst made the obvious suggestion that the dream had to do with learning to do what you do consciously. How much better it would be to learn that you needed the time alone and arrange your life so that was possible.

A few months later, I was working with my second analyst. With her help, I had clearly identified this area as a complex for me— this getting angry at people when they were sick. She suggested that it grew out of, in her deliciously strong language, my "being tyrannized in the house by illness as a child." I formed the pattern of hating illness and even, for a time, the person who was ill in response to these childhood experiences.

I was very excited when she said this, because it felt so accurate. Eagerly I asked her, "So what do I do now?" She said, "Oh, you just know it." I wanted to throw something at her, because it felt so inadequate. I thought it was nothing. Part of my subsequent discovery is that, though the problem of a complex is not solved simply by the knowing, knowing is much better than nothing.

She said that even after you know the symbolism and the reasons behind a complex, you are not rid of the complex. You still have it to deal with, though it does gradually fade with time and conscious work. We discussed various practical ways to deal with my new knowledge in relation to my husband and children, for example.

Then she took it to a somewhat deeper level by asking me about the family history. After I had told her stories about my father, grandfather, and great grandfather, she noted that there was a long family history of repressing naive, childlike spontaneity and that things which the ancestors do not live out are always a great weight on the children. In a number of ways I was the chosen child to live out some of the unfulfilled life of my fathers, for example, in going to law school, and this had drawn me away from my own true, spontaneous path. In fact, she said, one is capable of much more feeling and love to others when one is just recklessly oneself.

So for me at that point, in late 1965, I had the conscious awareness that the complex had a dual source. At the most obvious level, it spoke to my life experience with my father's headaches and how they tyrannized the family. On a deeper, family history or genogram level, it spoke to a long course of the repression of spontaneity. In the language I am suggesting in this book, I would now say that these insights had come to me by beginning with the core image of my emotional hatred for illness.

I had begun by focusing on the emotion I felt when the core image presented itself in my life situation. Then through following the trail from that emotion, through dream work and family history work, I had come to deeper insights about myself. By seeing my father's and grandfather's failure to live their true lives, I had come to see my need to learn to claim the "alone" time I needed in a conscious way, to honor my own spontaneity, and thus to live my life as truly as I could. Even in my family the rage at illness and the lack of spontaneity are obviously connected, I think, as I think the headaches themselves came from the failure to live truly.

I went along for a number of years working with this knowledge of my complex and its effects. A painful moment came to me one day when I had a terrible headache and realized that by my illness I was tyrannizing my family. It felt as if I had come full circle and I experienced the pain of seeing how I had become that which I hated. I was sick a lot as a child, first with recurring kidney infections and later with extreme nausea and pain in my menstrual cycle.

Another insight came to me a few years later when my mother said to me wistfully, "I guess it was terrible of me, but I never minded when you were sick, because then you stayed home and I had you all to myself." I felt a cold chill run down my back when she said it. My mother is a person who loves to nurture others, but I could feel that desire of hers not only positively, but in its dangerous, negative aspect.

I think her desire to have me at home had another source, though, which I saw when she told me, only two or three years ago, a story so poignant that my eyes filled with tears. It showed me a side of my mother I had never seen at all. She had been a school teacher when she got pregnant with me. In those days, a pregnant teacher was immediately fired, but her school asked her to stay on and then to come back as soon as she could to finish out the school year after my February birth.

I had heard that part of the story before. It had always made me feel quite proud of her, as I knew that she must have been very good to overcome the customs of the time in this way. The story she had never told was what happened to her the next September when she could hear through the open windows the shouts of school children starting back to school after the summer vacation. She wasn't going, but she must have felt a great longing to do so.

She told me that she cried, but she didn't want me to think that she begrudged me the care I needed from her. So she held me, with tears streaming down her face, and told me over and over that she really wanted me, loved me, and just sort of missed the excitement of the first day of school. I was only six months old, but who knows, really, what infants grasp of what they are told.

There was no thought in those days that a young mother would work while she had a baby at home. Getting to finish her school year was the anomaly. Reflecting on this story, I came to see that she had longed to keep working outside the home. She was really no more suited to homemaking than I am, but then no such thought was possible. So I think probably her wanting to keep me at home when I was just a little sick was an outcome of her own professional frustrations, and the cold chill that ran down my back reflected some of her unlived life which came down to me as well. I also saw that she always intended to set me free and let me go, but it was always hard for her.

Some years after my work in analysis, another powerful aspect of this core image of illness was connected for me with a memory of an early trauma, perhaps my earliest memory. I would not say that I had forgotten the incident in the intervening years; I simply never connected it with my own problems around illness.

Before I was three years old, my parents got so concerned about my continuing difficulty with breathing that they took me from the little country doctor who had been treating me to a specialist in Texarkana, the nearest city. He said that my tonsils and adenoids were so enlarged that I would probably die if they weren't removed. So they began to plan for that removal.

I had not liked being hurt by the city doctor at the hospital, and my folks just decided not to tell me beforehand about the operation which, they reasoned, I wouldn't have understood anyway. They just told me we were going to Texarkana, which I loved to do. So I was happy all the way to the moment when the car pulled up in front of the hospital. I evidently saw it and knew: that's where they hurt you.

What I can remember about it begins at that moment. I remember deciding that I wasn't going into the hospital. I remember fighting my parents and grandparents as all four adults tried to get me out of the car and I held on to the door facing, the windows, the handles, fighting and screaming all the time. I fought them all the way. They had to strap me down on the operating table and have extra nurses hold me. I remember it right up until the moment the ether began to take effect when I screamed for my grandmother's help one last despairing time.

My parents thought they were doing a right thing, as well as saving themselves some trouble, but they did neither one. When I connected this incident with my complex, I saw new aspects of this core image. It is not blaming my parents to say that this became for me a formative experience of betrayal which is paradigmatic of how I feel toward authority and also toward my growing up with a real difficulty going inside hospitals for any reason. It made me sick just to walk inside them.

As an adult, I know that my parents didn't betray me seriously in that incident, but the die was cast in my life, so to speak. I had begun to learn survival in a particular way: don't trust anyone; they may not be telling you the truth. Had I been able to use the language at two, I would probably have asked: where was God in my betrayal? Is anybody there? Does anybody care?

My own religious conversion began with learning to trust, first one person and then another, and then a few more, all in the context of a Christian church, from which I began to think maybe God could be trusted and to try that out. I began to surround myself with people who were trying to be absolutely honest, and I began to risk radical honesty myself.

Inherent in the image of that day in front of the hospital and my subsequent lack of trust is the way of healing the wound. I have to find people who will tell me the truth, no matter how painful. Beyond that, I have to find a God who can be trusted.

Looking back I could see that a main problem I had entering therapy was being able to trust myself to anyone. I had learned to trust my Christian friends, but was far less sure about analysts. During my first day's contact with analysts at the Jung Institute, I unexpectedly began to cry when one analyst I was interviewing mentioned my being afraid to trust anyone enough to enter analysis. That night I dreamed that I was working with her and noticed that she was off in a corner at a party whispering to people, as I feared, about me and my confidential discussions with her. My fear was imaged in the dream whispering. Actually, I think the dream may have had some objective commentary about that particular analyst as well.

Be that as it may, I think that for me the core image of illness and my negative reaction to it was closely allied in my three-year-old heart with betrayal and lack of trust of people. The intensity of my adult response to illness came directly from the connection with betrayal, so that as I moved through life, the emotions became so confused as to be difficult to distinguish. They were woven together for me and my emotional responses, but the identification of core images and insight into their connections can lead the way out. We even get attracted to connected areas for the healing of our wounds, as I was attracted to healing ministry.

During my years as a campus minister in a small liberal arts college, I participated enthusiastically for several years in planning and teaching in a wholistic health seminar, which emphasized ways in which patients could take more responsibility for their own health care and health care givers could be more sensitive in their treatment styles. I think something of a revolution in health care has taken place in the last twenty years or so, and my core image rage was put to good use to help educate my students toward that.

My two formative stories which I mentioned in the chapter on stories as parts of my own myth can also be seen as related to my core image. When life lands a nut on my head like Chicken Little, I probably feel like the helpless two year old, betrayed into the hands of those who can hurt you. That is one of my possible responses; and its best result comes when I get in touch with my inner Wise Old Owl: "Now wait a minute, Chicken Little, where were you standing when it hit?"

The other response is the little toy clown. When the train breaks down and all the dolls and toys begin to cry, I want to jump and say, "Cheer up, that's not the only engine in the world. Maybe someone else will help us." In other words, we will not always be betrayed; we are not helpless in the face of life.

These things are also very strange and deep. In 1987, I finally agreed to have a breast biopsy, as my doctor had been urging for some time. The biopsy was fine, but they almost lost the patient. As soon as they began giving me the general anesthetic, I stopped breathing, and they had considerable difficulty getting me started again. The anesthesiologist told me they were seconds from a tracheotomy when I finally breathed. I awoke with a black and blue chest cage and an extremely sore throat, and I now carry a notation on my medical records that I am allergic. Interesting word, "allergic," isn't it?

Yet I cannot escape the remarkable similarity between that experience and its timing and my earlier trauma with my tonsils. I don't understand that one, but I am taking it very seriously and waiting for whatever it has to teach me.

So there were some more layers which the core image of my trouble with illness have brought me to see. As is always the case, as I mentioned above, this configuration is also deeply involved with my images of God and God's relation to us. It does not seem an accident to me that I have ended up in healing work, but yet have a strong resistance to being fitted into other people's boxes. I want freedom for myself and others to be recklessly ourselves, and I believe it is pleasing to God when we are. I remember the Scottish runner in *Chariots of Fire* telling his sister that it was God who made him fast, and when I run, he said, I can feel his pleasure.

Another side of my concern with illness and with God has been the problem of theodicy, the relationship of good and evil, which has been called the primary problem religious people have to struggle with in this century. I have probably preached more sermons on this subject than any other; I can find a theodicy issue in almost any text! This is probably my ultimate theological issue, and for me it is probably best worded in this question: can God be trusted?

This is a very old issue, of course, and one of the hardest to make peace with. As Archibald Macleish puts it in *J.B.*, if God is God, he can't be good; if God is good, he can't be God. After the holocaust and the other horrors of the twentieth century, a common question is: where was God? Where is God?

It is also an ancient question, of course. It is instructive how many times the psalmists ask it: " Why dost thou stand afar off, O Lord? Why dost thou hide thyself in times of trouble?" (10:1) "How long, O Lord? Wilt thou forget me for ever? How long wilt thou hide thy face from me? How long must I bear pain in my soul, and have sorrow in my heart all the day?" (13:1–2) "My God, my God, why hast thou forsaken me? Why art thou so far from helping me, from the words of my groaning? O my God, I cry by day, but thou dost not answer; and by night, but find no rest." (22:1–2) And on and on.

Part of the answer to this question, the faith answer, is confirmed by twentieth-century depth psychology. That is the answer which says, as I have been suggesting, that the answer to life's healing and wholeness lies in the presence of grace at the very point of wounding. The possibility of redemption and healing is in the core image itself; God is there. In the ancient formula, whatever the world, the flesh, and the devil have to offer, God is there.

·10·

Conclusion:
Of God and Our
Common Life

*F*inding our core images is part of becoming aware of the narrative stories of our lives. Many people express fear that such attention to our own lives is self-serving, selfish, self-absorbed. "Navel gazing" is the sneering phrase used to discount such work. That great, human, funny teacher of souls, Teresa of Avila, though, said that the only room in the "Interior Castle" that we never leave behind and always need to return to is the room of self-knowledge, where we learn true humility by seeing ourselves as we really are. It has always seemed to me that she put the modern criticism of inner work in its proper place by this remark. She sees that true self-knowledge leads to humility, not self-satisfaction. People who want to stay satisfied with themselves will do well to avoid the room of self-knowledge.

Of course, if we stay only in that one room forever, the sneering criticism is valid. Humility itself comes from seeing accurately—neither in self-satisfaction nor self-hatred. We are not all good or all bad; we are all a bit of both. Seeing ourselves more clearly, we see our choices more clearly. That is where the living quality of our images is so important; they are to lead us on into life, our common life, which can be lived with fuller awareness, consciousness, and purpose.

One of the best statements of the deeper meaning of exploring our own stories comes from Frederick Buechner speaking about his own embarrassment at writing an autobiography. Buechner argues that, far from being selfish, we may in fact be listening to the voice of God when we reflect on our own lives. I quote from it at length because it addresses this problem with precision and integrity. Though he was somewhat embarrassed, he decided:

> But I do it anyway. I do it because it seems to me that no matter who you are, and no matter how eloquent or otherwise, if you tell your own story with sufficient candor and concreteness, it will be an interesting story and in some sense a universal story. I do it in the hope of encouraging others to do the same—at least to look back over their own lives, as I have looked back over mine, for certain themes and patterns and signals that are so easy to miss when you're caught up in the process of living them. If God speaks to us at all other than through such official channels as the Bible and the church, then I think that he speaks to us largely through what happens to us, so what I have done both in this book and in its predecessor is to listen back over what has happened to me—as I hope my readers may be moved to listen back over what has happened to them— for the sound, above all else, of his voice.
>
> Because the word that God speaks to us is always an incarnate word—a word spelled out to us not alphabetically, in syllables, but enigmatically, in events, even in the books we read and the movies we see—the chances are we will never get it just right. We are so used to hearing what we want to hear and remaining deaf to what it would be well for us to hear that it is hard to break the habit. But if we keep our hearts and minds open as well as our ears, if we listen with patience and hope, if we remember at all deeply and honestly, then I think we come to recognize, beyond all doubt, that, however faintly we may hear him, he is indeed speaking to us, and that, however little we may understand of it, his word to each of us is both recoverable and precious beyond telling. In that sense autobiography becomes a way of praying, and a book like this, if it matter at all, matters mostly as a call to prayer.[1]

In his comments on lectures he gave at Harvard, he further reinforces this position:

> In writing those lectures and the book they later turned into, it

came to seem to me that if I were called upon to state in a few words the essence of everything I was trying to say both as a novelist and as a preacher, it would be something like this: Listen to your life. See it for the fathomless mystery that it is. In the boredom and pain of it no less than in the excitement and gladness: touch, taste, smell your way to the holy and hidden heart of it because in the last analysis all moments are key moments, and life itself is grace.[2]

Buechner there stresses another aspect of work with our lives—the mystery which will never be completely fathomed, partly because of our limitations, but also partly because it is living, changing, growing, never static, even in times of apparent rest. The beauty of seeing mystery in life is caught in a statement attributed to Einstein:

The most beautiful thing we can experience is the mysterious. It is the source of all true art and science. He to whom this emotion is a stranger, who can no longer pause to wonder and stand wrapt in awe, is as good as dead.[3]

One way to reclaim the mystery is through this process of listening to our lives. As has been apparent throughout, operating as a Christian theist like Buechner, I connect this mystery of life with God. So much depends upon the place where we begin, the world view from which we make our theories, diagnoses, and treatment plans. My place is within a largely traditional Christian faith, and I have tried to be open about that, so that readers may know my bias and make their own adaptations accordingly. As I have said, I do not think core image work is limited to those in Christianity, but others have to do their own sorting to claim what is useful for them.

Some psychological theorists have given us useful information about the formation of our relation to the mystery of life, and it can thus prove helpful to look at some of the relationships between psychology and religion with reference to God, gods, and god-image (or imago). Operationally, our mental pictures of God are significant core images, and I have referred throughout this work to the relation between one's core images and one's personal image of God.

Scriptural tradition is replete with images of God. Repeatedly, both in the Greek and Hebrew scriptures, runs the theme that no one can see God and live; this is part of the terror Jesus' apostles experienced as they began to believe him to be God incarnate. Yet for us to be in relationship with God, we must do so through an image, even including the image of imagelessness. Some of these images speak with more power to one, others to another person. None is completely adequate.

Psychology in its study of human experience, inevitably runs into this question of human and divine. The answers which different theorists give by way of explaining (or, in some instances, explaining away) images of God are varied. Several factors enter into the intersection between psychology and theology, and I will try briefly to sketch a few of them in the context of the history of modern psychology and then elaborate some of the connections I see operating.

Some relevant factors are: the nature of various god-images themselves; the assessment of whether god-images are creative or destructive in human life; the source for the particular god-images of a particular person; the assessment of whether an individual's images represent pathology or health; the assessment of whether an image is "real" or "imagined"; and the existence or not of a God behind or beyond the god-images.

Psychology has frequently had a bad name with religious people, in large part I think because of Freud's teaching that religion was an immature sickness from which we needed to be cured. Freud felt that the imago of God ("the dark power of Destiny") grew directly out of the parents, particularly the "father in the flesh." He believed that God was only a projection, not an objective reality, and that in the end only people who remained children continued to believe in God. In fact, I think it is fair to say that he turned traditional religious orthodoxy on its head. Tradition says (in many world religions) that God created humanity; Freud said human beings create God.

Jung broke with Freud for other reasons, but he also viewed our relation to God somewhat differently. He treated issues about God at length; there are over ten columns in the index to his *Collected Works* covering references to God, gods, and god-image. Jung repeatedly urged that he only reported empirically that a god-image was present in the psyche, which contained a reality, even a purposive reality, but he claimed not to be able to make statements about the reality of God outside the psyche, either "for" or "against." On the reality of the unseen he was much more adamant. He said only ignorance denies it.

Because of this and because he at least said he was unsure about the objective existence of God, not absolutely certain like Freud, his psychology has been welcomed by many in religious circles. His personality theory allows for the validity of religious experience, even its positive role in human life, in a way which Freud did not. He offers a methodology for exploring god-images without negating the possibility of God, and in fact even helps us expand our notions of the unending variety of ways God appears and speaks to us.

There are many Christians, though, who welcome Jungian theory no more than they do Freudian, some even feeling his teachings are against Christianity. I do not think this is a fair assessment, but it is also clear that Jungian orthodoxy is different from Christian orthodoxy in several important aspects. For the purposes of work with core images, I think the primary difference lies in the perceived source of guidance or "calling" forward in our lives. Jungian orthodoxy recognizes—apparently—no higher authority than the messages from the unconscious, to be mediated in turn by the conscious point of view; and many Jungian analysts will so assert. Jung's theory would thus share with many other psychologies the view that morality is relative, to be determined individually.

I say "apparently" because Jung himself is said to have commented that even if he thought the unconscious "told" him to kill someone, he would not do so. That moral reluctance on his part, as stated in his own example, must come from some other standard—from what has been called "borrowed capital"—from the standards taught in the Jewish and Christian faiths which lie behind the European culture in which he was nurtured.[4] At his clearest, however, Jung refuses to say whether the "imprint" of God on the psyche (which he observed) also has an "imprinter" behind it, though he seems to assume that it does. I think we can welcome his expansion of the understanding of personality without requiring that a particular religious orthodoxy be espoused.

Freud's denigration of religious ideas as belonging to the childish phase of life had led to religion's being largely ignored by his later disciples, until one loyal follower of his, Ana-Maria Rizzuto, suggested a correction of Freud. Working from the object relations school of psychoanalysis, Rizzuto stressed that each person's image of God needs to be respectfully considered from the point of view of the person.[5] She suggests that there is no such thing as a person without a God representation and that there is no reason why this information is not as relevant as any other. She further theorized that these images came from a variety of sources in each persons's life, not always simply in the pattern perceived in the person's father. In fact, in the United States today, some research indicates that the mother image is more frequently projected onto God.[6]

Of the actual existence of God, Rizzuto said psychology could not try to answer that question, could not "make pronouncements," leaving such speculation to philosophers and theologians. One of her major contributions has been her respectful attitude toward religion, and her honoring of individuals by attention to their religious quests has been welcomed by religious scholars.

John McDargh, also working from an object relations perspective, sees a major paradigm shift from psychoanalytic theory to psychoanalytic object relations theory, one which says that human beings are primarily motivated by the need to be in relationships which confirm them and thus confirm their right to exist. These relationships can continue to grow and change, and the same is true for representations of God and god-images.[7]

McDargh has further researched how the images of God and faith work in our lives with a backdrop of faith development stages on the one hand and transference theory on the other. He gives us insight into how some of these images are distorted in the way they become internalized for each of us and how those distortions can be worked with. He too makes the point that we can work with these images psychologically and understand their sources.

He goes further than Rizzuto when he also stresses that we need to approach these images of God with a measure of modesty and awe, because we can never know "how it may happen that *God* may be a source for the sense of God" (emphasis added).[8] "Simply because the foundation is so located [in early life experience] does not mortgage the individual to that heritage or that God any more than an individual's relationship with his or her own parents necessarily need be frozen forever in the condition of childhood."⁹ God who makes all things new, McDargh suggests, can also be seen "correcting, enlarging, and re-forming the imagings of our heart." This is another way of honoring the mystery behind the symbol which honors the individual soul and its God.

Joann Wolski Conn uses Kegan's constructive developmental theory to talk about the discernment of the level of spiritual maturity which a person's image of God indicates. She mentions, for example, that if "one is developing a sense of herself or himself as free and self-directed, then she or he must relate to a God who affirms and empowers that freedom if she or he is to preserve that self-identity."¹⁰ The way beyond childlike dependence, Conn suggests, involves moving beyond projections of a paternalistic or maternalistic God who treats adults like children.

I have mentioned in several examples how the individual's image of God relates to the core image, both in being affected by the traumas of the image and in the redemptive possibilities to which the image points. "A person's erroneous view of self is interwoven with that person's erroneous view of God."¹¹ From a theistic view these erroneous views of God can be seen as the idolatry which lies at the heart of most psychological pathology, as people have made relative values into absolute idols.

Yet if we are ever to get beyond childlike dependence or idolatrous gods, we must begin with honesty about the place where we are. "If we are ever to reach through our God-images to the God who breaks all our images, then we must begin with our own pictures for God—noticing them, embracing them, housing them." This is the only way we can avoid the twin dangers of losing the sense of a true, living, connection with a God who is more than just words, on the one hand, or getting lost in the literalism of our god-images on the other.¹²

Furthermore, an image which speaks deeply to one person may be quite destructive for another. John McDargh cites an interesting example, that of Brian, a young seminarian, engaged in compulsive confession, eventually to the point where he went to confession daily. When challenged, Brian said he only felt close to God right after confession. Subsequent psychotherapy revealed that Brian's father only related to him when he would come home from work and punish Brian for something he had done. As McDargh says,

"Brian's God representation, not too surprisingly, was one in which intimacy was only possible through the dynamics of sin and forgiveness."[13] Realizing this and mourning his genuine neglect by his father enabled Brian to come to more developed images of God as friend.

No matter how "accurate" or "mature" an image of God is, the world's theistic religions assert that the image is less than the true God. Imagination theory further informs us that we are dependent on what images are available to us, so we must find an image which can anchor our experience of faith so that it becomes for us a symbol to key our pattern of meaning.[14] For example, I have found a lot of difficulty preaching to an American audience about the significance of God as "king." "Lord," one of our most common scriptural images of God, has surely lost its original meaning for most modern people. For purposes of core image work, what we need to remember is that no symbol is adequate for everyone, no matter how much it is found in scripture.

I remember when I first learned this. I had personally been moved by the nurturing closeness of our relationship to God suggested by Jesus' continuing use of the image "father" for God. Then I saw how destructive this was for a Christian friend of mine. Her father had refused to let her get the education for which she longed, so she left home. When he was dying, she went back to his bedside and asked for his forgiveness. Even though he knew he was dying, he said no. For her, "father" was someone who refuses to forgive you on his deathbed, when you have really done nothing wrong. Hardly what Jesus meant! Yet if even well-meaning Christian folk would require her to accept the "father" designation for God in order to worship the "true" God, they would be doing her and the church a grave disservice.

An even more powerful expression of this difficulty was captured by the pseudonymous author of a book of poems about the author's experience of incest committed by her father. The poem is called "God":

> I've been glad for God the Spirit
> and for God the Son
> because I don't believe
> my heart can ever understand

that God
is like a father.[15]

Precisely the opposite effect was experienced by a woman whose natural father abandoned the family and whose subsequent step-fathers abused her severely, with the permission or even collusion of her mother. However, she later attended a Lutheran church where she heard that God the father loved us unconditionally, and despite all her "fatherly" and parental evidence to the contrary, she believed that message. For her the ability to image a loving father transcended her personal parental experience, and she internalized that image of God and was consistently sustained by God's love through a very difficult childhood and adolescence.

The difficulty of making the distinction between the reality of God as experienced in given images is currently a hot battle among Christians, particularly with reference to gender-related images. The recent focus on feminine images of God has been a saving grace to many—women and men—in freeing them from exclusively masculine images which were destructive for them in their connotations. For others, the feminine images are destructive, and for them, forcing feminine image patterns is unhelpful. Perhaps it will be impossible for some time to come for us to assess gender-related language of God. Krister Stendahl suggests that stories, from Jesus' parables to rabbi's stories, all funny, are the primary way we can keep ourselves from thinking we can accurately image God.[16]

There are no universal rules in God imagery, but there are the possibilities of growth and development in and through the images. The faith development material points to patterns which can be discerned in the movements and changes in our images of God. The images can move from a distant, literal, anthropomorphic God to images of transcendent mystery and co-creation, sometimes breaking out of culture-bound images.[17] Core image work, as I have mentioned in several of the examples, can also be a source for finding larger pictures of God if "our God is too small."

New images of God which carry grace and healing often come to individuals to bring balance to their lives. I most easily get caught these days in overscheduling and a rather compulsive busyness. It came to me once on a retreat that a primary healing image of God for me is what I call a "deep chuckle," as if God invites me to let my intensity be punctured by a humorous perspective on the relative importance of my worries and opinions. It's as if God speaks to me like the Wise Owl saying to Chicken Little, "Laugh, Chicken Little, and we will too"—never *at* me in ridicule, but *with* me. It's an invitation to delight and joy—an invitation to calm down and just be for a while instead of being caught in such a flurry of doing.

The vessels to hold the experiences of life, this life itself of grace, the core images, whether images of God or others, though they may come to us in part from our personal life experience, are incomplete when they are only individual. We need to look at our own images of God, but we also need to look at the "official god-images offered by tradition," for otherwise we risk claiming our own images as a new official one. As the Ulanovs point out, "The religious imagination always . . . makes us ask how the old official pictures of God touch, inform, confront our personal god-images, and how our own images touch, confront, inform those of tradition." They add, "We have our own images and they are precious, but they need much more nourishment than they can bring with them to grow large enough to house the spirit. Our images are little. Tradition is large."[18]

Religious experience, like all of our lives, needs also to be socialized—in family or church or some place where we can find a shared symbol system. We are social creatures, and we cannot simply separate ourselves into our own individual lives. All our lives affect one another—consciously or unconsciously, for good or ill.

This is the area Wallace and I wrote about in *The Hero Journey in Dreams* in the chapter on the return of the hero with the treasure to the community. We bring our gifts and we receive the support of others who share sufficiently in our symbol systems so that we can understand and help one another. It is the social healing which twelve-step programs are pointing us toward, and their rapid proliferation is telling us something important. So, though my focus here is on the individual's images (and I do believe that is the necessary beginning place), I think we live into our life's meaning more completely in our wider contexts.

Our personal images, though very much ours, have also a shared life with others, which comes simply from our common humanity. If we are cut, we bleed; tears reflect strong emotion, whether the cause is trivial or childish or profound.

My experience with core images that are genuinely worked through and responsibly lived with is that they lead us back to our common human lives without our straining after social significance. We are social beings and we yearn for community and significance when we are healed enough and whole enough to come to the world of others without overwhelming fear. We can have the courage to be vulnerable to the world's wounds when we have ministered to our own, and this courage can be fulfilled in our particular vocation to the world, not one that someone else has laid on us or one that is another person's vocation we try to ape.

So I see this work with images as the personal building blocks which can help both us and the culture become socially whole. A dream image which pictures this relationship was shared with me several years ago. The dreamer, a fifty-year-old religious sister, dreamed it the night before a retreat:

> I am out in beautiful country, blue skies, large green mountains—beauty all around me. There are hundreds and hundreds of children. A woman comes and organizes us into rows. We are all holding hands. The children open the semi-circles of rows to make room for more. I am standing in the first row at the end.
>
> After everybody is in position overlooking the mountains, the woman teaches us a single melody—two notes (re-do). We are to sing in rounds. The words to the melody is our own name. Everyone sings their own name.
>
> We begin the round and it is amazing how quickly we all learn to sing. Magnificent music—hundreds of voices and all in harmony. . . .
>
> I do notice that we are all singing our own name, yet it sounds like one. There is unison, harmony. . . .
>
> The singing never stops.

That's it. That's how it is. When we all truly sing our own names, it is magnificent and it is harmony. Anyone who has worked with dreams will not be surprised to learn that another part of this sister's dream also included some specific applications of this image of harmony to the disharmonies in the dreamer's own context— those people and structures which discounted her "name" and its singing. The dream thus in a very practical way gave her both a pointer to the specific "crunch" areas in her life *and* a visionary image of the transcendent harmony to be lived toward.

Mysteriously, wonderfully, the healing images are presented to us, and at the beginning they are frequently perceived as destructive. Yet when they are lived into, in all the myriad ways that our theology and psychology teach us, sometimes we begin to see that other side of the images. Something destructive in our lives can begin to be transformed into its opposite. Core images are like the fabled leprechauns, who, if you can catch them and hold on to them despite all their tricks and deceptions and shape changing, then will eventually lead you to the pot of gold at the end of the rainbow.

When we can use core images this way, we in helping professions are helping those who come to us to make the volcanoes of their lives from islands into peninsulas and continents. And I haven't even mentioned another faith position of mine: that once we learn to listen for the symbolic images and patterns, the people who come to us are the very people whom we can help and from whom we can learn something new.

I really do think it is all a wonderful plan, as if a great computer in the sky is matching us all up, so we can all discover that we are none of us islands unto ourselves. That, for me, is the spirit in which counseling can flourish to the edifying of the world and the building up of the body of those who are coming awake.

Notes

Chapter 1. Symbols and Personality

1. Ann and Barry Ulanov, *The Healing Imagination: The Meeting of Psyche and Soul* (New York: Paulist Press, 1991), p. 39.

2. For a more detailed discussion of symbols and images and how they work, see Jean Dalby Clift and Wallace B. Clift, *Symbols of Transformation in Dreams* (New York: Crosroad, 1985).

3. Douglas McGaughey, "Through Myth to Imagination," *Journal of the American Academy of Religion* 56, no.1 (Spring, 1988): 51–76.

4. C. G. Jung and M.-L. von Franz, eds., *Man and His Symbols* (Garden City, N.Y.: Doubleday, 1964), p. 21.

5. Viktor E. Frankl, *Man's Search for Meaning: An Introduction to Logotherapy* (New York: Washington Square Press, 1963), p. 104.

6. Aarne Siirala, *The Voice of Illness: A Study in Therapy and Prophecy* (Philadelphia: Fortress Press, 1964).

Chapter 2. Early Memories

1. Frederick Buechner, *The Sacred Journey* (San Francisco: Harper & Row, 1982), p. 21.

2. John D. Barbour, "Character and Characterization in Religious Autobiography," *Journal of the American Academy of Religion* 55, no. 2 (Summer 1987): 324.

Chapter 3. Community and Family

1. C. G. Jung, *Letters*, vol. 1: 1906–1950, trans. R. F. C. Hull (Princeton, N.J.: Princeton University Press, 1973), p.436.

2. Linda Schierse Leonard, *Witness to the Fire: Creativity and the Veil of Addiction* (Boston: Shambhala, 1989), p. xiv.

3. Ibid., p. xv.

4. Don S. Browning, "The Pastoral Counselor as Ethicist: What Difference Do We Make?" *Criterion* 29, no. 3 (Autumn 1990): 11.

5. W. Hugh Missildine, *Your Inner Child of the Past* (New York: Simon and Schuster, 1963).

6. Alice Miller, *The Drama of the Gifted Child*, trans. Ruth Ward (New York: Basic Books, 1981); *For Your Own Good*, trans. Hildegarde and Hunter Hannum (New York: Farrar, Straus & Giroux, 1983).

7. Heinz Kohut, *Self Psychology and the Humanities: Reflections on a New Psychoanalytic Approach* (New York: W. W. Norton, 1985), pp. 115ff.

8. William F. Nerin, *Family Reconstruction: Long Day's Journey Into Light* (New York: W. W. Norton, 1986).

Chapter 4. Stories and Songs

1. William Butler Yeats, quoted by Justin Kaplan in "The Naked Self and Other Problems," in *Telling Lives: The Biographer's Art*, ed. M. Pachter (Philadelphia: University of Pennsylvania Press, 1985), p. 46.

2. C. G. Jung, *Symbols of Transformation*, trans. R. F. C. Hull, vol. 5 of *The Collected Works of C. G. Jung* (Princeton, N.J.: Princeton University Press, 1956), p. xxiv.

3. Rollo May, *The Cry for Myth* (New York: W. W. Norton, 1991), pp. 9, 20–21.

4. Jean Dalby Clift and Wallace B. Clift, *The Hero Journey in Dreams* (New York: Crossroad, 1988), pp. 3–9.

5. Bruno Bettelheim, *The Uses of Enchantment: The Meaning and Importance of Fairy Tales* (New York: Alfred A. Knopf, 1977), p. 152.

6. *John Thomson's Modern Course for the Piano: The Second Grade Book* (Cincinnati, Ohio: Willis Music Co., 1937), p. 17.

7. Marguerite Henry, *Brighty of the Grand Canyon* (New York: Scholastic Book Services, 1953).

8. Linda T. Sanford, *Strong at the Broken Places: Overcoming the Trauma of Childhood Abuse* (New York: Avon Books, 1990), p. 6.

Chapter 5. Dreams

1. C. G. Jung, *The Symbolic Life*, trans. R. F. C. Hull, vol. 18 of *The Collected Works of C. G. Jung* (Princeton, N.J.: Princeton University Press, 1976), par. 248.

2. *The Confessions of Augustine in Modern English*, trans. Sherwood Eliot Wirt (Grand Rapids, Mich.: Zondervan, 1971), p. 46.

3. Ibid.

4. Sister Miriam Therese Winter, "The Wedding Banquet, *"Joy Is Like the Rain* (New York: Vanguard Music Corp., 1965), p. 22.

Chapter 6. *Operational Theory*

1. *Silent Fire: An Invitation to Western Mysticism*, ed. Walter Holden Capps and Wendy M. Wright (San Francisco: Harper & Row, 1978), p. 7.

2. Paul W. Pruyser, *The Minister as Diagnostician: Personal Problems in Pastoral Perspective* (Philadelphia: Westminster Press, 1976), pp. 76–78.

3. Bede Frost, *The Art of Mental Prayer* (London: SPCK, 1954), p. 213.

4. Alan Jones, *Exploring Spiritual Direction* (San Francisco: Harper & Row, 1982), p. 82.

5. Pierre de Bérulle, *La Direction Spirituelle*, chap. 1, cited in Frost, *The Art of Mental Prayer.*

6. F. Augustine Baker, *Holy Wisdom* (New York: Harper and Brothers, 1876, ed. from 1657 by Rt. Rev. Abbot Sweeney), p. 35.

7. Roberto Assagioli, *Psychosynthesis: A Manual of Principles and Techniques* (New York: Penguin Books, 1976), pp. 4, 182ff.

8. Virginia M. Axline, *Play Therapy* (New York: Ballantine Books, 1947), pp. 62, 98.

9. Sharon Parks, "Meaning and Symbol in Constructive Developmental Perspective," *Pastoral Psychology* 33, no. 2 (Winter 1984): 64–73.

10. Rodney J. Hunter, ed., *Dictionary of Pastoral Care and Counseling* (Nashville: Abingdon Press, 1990), pp. 423–24.

11. R. D. Laing, *The Divided Self: An Existential Study in Sanity and Madness* (Baltimore: Penguin Books, 1959), p. 12.

12. Mary Barnes and Joseph Berke, *Mary Barnes: Two Accounts of a Journey Through Madness* (New York: Harcourt Brace Jovanovich, 1971), pp. 80, 87, 351.

13. John Weir Perry, *The Far Side of Madness* (Englewood Cliffs, N.J.: Prentice-Hall, 1974); *Roots of Renewal in Myth and Madness: The Meaning of Psychotic Episodes* (San Francisco: Jossey-Bass Pubs., 1976); *The Heart of History* (Albany, N.Y.: State University of New York Press, 1987).

14. *The Varieties of Religious Experience* (1902: reprint, New York: Penguin Books, 1982), pp. 508.

15. Walter E. Conn, "Pastoral Counseling for Self-Transcendence: The Integration of Psychology and Theology," *Pastoral Psychology* 36, no. 1 (Fall 1987): 29–48.

16. Terry D. Cooper, "Carl Rogers and Martin Luther—A 'Reformation' in the Helping Professions," *Pastoral Psychology* 38, no. 1 (Fall 1989): 15–24.

17. Ibid., p. 24.

18. C. G. Jung, *Memories, Dreams, Reflections* (New York: Vintage Books, 1961), p. 150.

Chapter 7. Diagnosis

1. Pruyser, *The Minister as Diagnostician*, p. 30.
2. Joseph B. Wheelwright, *St. George and the Dandelion* (San Francisco: C. G. Jung Institute of San Francisco, 1982), pp. 29–30.
3. C. G. Jung, *The Psychogenesis of Mental Disease*, trans. R. F. C. Hull, vol. 3 of *The Collected Works of C. G. Jung* (New York: Pantheon Books, 1960), par. 539.
4. Douglas P. Hobson and Mel Jacob, "Possibilities and Pitfalls of Pastoral Diagnosis," *Pastoral Psychology* 34. no. 1 (Fall 1985): 30–41.
5. Pruyser, *The Minister as Diagnostician*, p. 61.
6. Personal Narrative Group, eds., *Interpreting Women's Lives: Feminist Theory and Personal Narratives* (Bloomington: Indiana University Press, 1989), p. 4.
7. C. G. Jung, *The Structure and Dynamics of the Psyche*, trans. R. F. C. Hull, vol. 8 of *The Collected Works of C. G. Jung* (New York: Pantheon Books, 1960), par. 201.
8. Robert Kegan, *The Evolving Self: Problem and Process in Human Development* (Cambridge, Mass.: Harvard University Press, 1982).
9. Joann Wolski Conn, *Spirituality and Personal Maturity* (New York: Paulist Press, 1989).
10. "The Problem of Universal and Particular in Structural Developmental Theory" (paper given to Religion and Social Sciences Section, American Academy of Religion, New Orleans, 19 November 1990).
11. Merle R. Jordan, *Taking on the Gods: The Task of the Pastoral Counselor* (Nashville: Abingdon Press, 1986), pp. 30–34.
12. Jim Amundsen, "The Self Psychological Vision of Cure" (workshop conducted at annual meeting of American Association of Pastoral Counselors, Minneapolis, 28 April 1985).
13. Kathleen V. Hurley and Theodore E. Dobson, *What's My Type?* (San Francisco: Harper, 1991), p. 2.
14. June Singer, "The Education of the Analyst," in *Jungian Analysis*, ed. Murray Stein (La Salle, Ill.: Open Court, 1982), p. 381.

Chapter 8. Treatment Planning

1. Lecture, American Association of Pastoral Counselors Annual Meeting, New Orleans, 1 May 1987.
2. C. G. Jung, *Freud and Psychoanalysis*, trans. R. F. C. Hull, vol. 4 of *The Collected Works of C. G. Jung* (New York: Pantheon Books, 1961), par. 408.

3. C. G. Jung, *The Symbolic Life*, par. 148.

4. C. G. Jung, *The Structure and Dynamics of the Psyche*, par. 590–91.

5. Jung and von Franz, *Man and His Symbols*, p. 161.

6. Jones, *Exploring Spiritual Direction*, p. 23.

7. Monica McGoldrick and Randy Gerson, *Genograms in Family Assessment* (New York: W. W. Norton, 1985).

8. My favorite is J. C. Cooper, *An Illustrated Encyclopaedia of Traditional Symbols* (London: Thames and Hudson, 1978), which is thorough and responsible without being overwhelming. In the overwhelming category I would place probably the most complete such dictionary ever compiled: Ad de Vries, *Dictionary of Symbols and Imagery* (Amsterdam: North-Holland Publishing Co., rev. ed., 1976). A handy small dictionary is *The Herder Symbol Dictionary*, trans. Boris Matthews (Wilmette, Ill.: Chiron Pubns., 1978). J. E. Cirlot, *A Dictionary of Symbols*, trans. Jack Sage (New York: Philosophical Library, 1962), was an early entry. It is good, though not as helpful, I think, as the others mentioned. A wonderful resource for amplification is *An Encyclopedia of Archetypal Symbolism*, ed. Beverly Moon, (Boston: Shambhala, 1991), a massive, incomparable work using 120 full-page color photographs from the Archive for Research in Archetypal Symbolism and commenting on them both historically and archetypally. For a feminist dictionary, you might like to use Barbara G. Walker, *The Woman's Encyclopedia of Myths and Secrets* (San Francisco: Harper & Row, 1983), which, though biased itself, does help to dispel the unconscious masculine bias of other dictionaries. Some kind of mythological encyclopedia can also be of help. One I have used is *Funk & Wagnalls Standard Dictionary of Folklore, Mythology and Legend*, ed. Maria Leach (San Francisco: Harper & Row, 1972).

9. Robert A. Johnson, *Inner Work: Using Dreams and Active Imagination for Personal Growth* (San Francisco: Harper & Row, 1986).

10. Ira Progoff, *At a Journal Workshop: The Basic Text and Guide for Using the Intensive Journal* (New York: Dialogue House Library, 1975); *The Practice of Process Meditation: The Intensive Journal Way to Spiritual Experience* (New York: Dialogue House Library, 1980).

11. Eugene T. Gendlin, *Focusing* (New York: Bantam Books, 2d rev. ed., 1981), p. 8.

12. August Lageman, "Family Systems Dynamics in Individual Therapy" (workshop, American Association of Pastoral Counselors Annual Meeting, St. Louis, 8 April 1989).

13. James W. Jones, "The Relational Self: Contemporary Psychoanalysis Reconsiders Religion," *Journal of the American Academy of Religion* 59, no. 1 (Spring 1991): 119–35.

14. Johnson, *Inner Work*, p. 98.

15. Elizabeth C. Cameron, "Creative Ritual: Bridge Between Mastery and Meaning," *Pastoral Psychology* 40, no. 1 (Fall 1991): 3–13.

Chapter 9. Working Through Case Material

1. Jordan, *Taking on the Gods*, pp. 78–79.
2. C. S. Lewis, *The Screwtape Letters* (New York: Macmillan, 1944), pp. 86–89.

Chapter 10. Conclusion: Of God and Our Common Life

1. *Now and Then* (San Francisco: Harper & Row, 1983), pp. 2–3.
2. Ibid., p. 87.
3. Quoted in Arthur C. Clarke, *The Ghost from the Grand Banks* (New York: Bantam Books, 1990), p. 129.
4. Wallace B. Clift, *Jung and Christianity: The Challenge of Reconciliation* (New York: Crossroad, 1982), p. 144.
5. Ana-Maria Rizzuto, *The Birth of the Living God: A Psychoanalytic Study* (Chicago: University of Chicago Press, 1979).
6. Jordan, *Taking on the Gods*, p. 30.
7. John McDargh, "Clues to Transcendence: Psychoanalytic Object Relations Theory On the Trail of the Mystery," (Lecture given at American Association of Pastoral Counselors Annual Meeting, Williamsburg, 18 May 1989).
8. John McDargh, *Psychoanalytic Object Relations Theory and the Study of Religion: On Faith and the Imaging of God* (Lanham, Md.: University Press of America, 1983), p. 245.
9. John McDargh, "God, Mother and Me: An Object Relational Perspective on Religious Material," *Pastoral Psychology* 34, no. 4 (Summer 1986): 251–63.
10. Wolski Conn, *Spirituality and Personal Maturity*, p. 111.
11. Jordan, *Taking on the Gods*, p. 24.
12. Ann Belford Ulanov, *Picturing God* (Cambridge, Mass.: Cowley Pubns., 1986), pp. 165–69.
13. McDargh, "God, Mother and Me," pp. 261–62.
14. Parks, "Meaning and Symbol in Constructive Developmental Perspective," pp. 66–67.
15. Martha Janssen, *Silent Scream* (Philadelphia: Fortress Press, 1983), p. 107.
16. Krister Stendahl, "The Language of the Bible and The Language of the Now" (lectures given at the Iliff School of Theology, 1–3 July 1980).
17. Fredrica R. Halligan and John J. Shea, "Sacred Images in Dreamwork: The Journey into Self as Journey into God," *Pastoral Psychology* 40, no. 1 (Fall 1991): 29–38.
18. Ann and Barry Ulanov, *The Healing Imagination*, pp. 31–32.

Index